Nursing - My Heartbeat

Dollicia Green
ARNP, MSN, FNP-BC, LNC

Table of Contents

Nursing - My Heartbeat

Acknowledgements

Faith, Family, Love in that order. To my Father in heaven thank you for seeing a purpose in me when I did not see a purpose in myself. Thank you for all the adversities that you empowered me to overcome. I pray that my hands help with healing, my compassion brings understanding and my heart brings comfort. Amen

Special "Thank You" to my Husband Darren Green thank you for your love and support. To my children Jaleesa, Dijon, Jada and Janae thank you. You give me life and your love is fuel for my determination to win.

To all my Family and Friends, I love you and I thank you for laughing, crying, praying and rejoicing with me all these years. I am so grateful that you are a part of my life.

To my triad (Mom, Aunt and Grandmother) I miss you more than words could ever express. Thank you for being a positive force in my life.

Dollicia

Nursing- My Heartbeat

By Dollicia Green, ARNP, MSN, FNP-BC, LNC

I'm about to tell you a story. It's the story of not just how I achieved my dream of becoming a nurse, but of the circumstances that made me the exact nurse that I was meant to be. Because yes - I listen to your heartbeat, but I also listen to the intention behind your words when you make a comment. I do care that you have all the information about your treatment, but I also care about what you're feeling inside. I'll gladly accept your intake forms, but I also accept you for exactly who you are at the moment I meet you. And of course, I love to send you out the door healthy and safe, but I also love when you arrive – not because there's obviously something wrong with your physical body to bring you in, but because I am so happy to make your acquaintance and to be in this amazing position to help.

As tough things happen in our lives, sometimes we wish that things were different or easier. It's hard not to wonder what life would be like if we had the devoted father we wanted or how great things would be if we were born into a rich family right from the start. And although some days; it seems like we'd trade anything to be in someone else's shoes; - someone who's a little luckier, or a little more attractive, or someone with a few more connections. I would never want that type of wish to come true. What we're actually seeking in those moments isn't really about the circumstances. It's about being recognized for who we are. When we wish to be someone else, it's because our own inner light is feeling dim. Our situation has gotten us down. We feel like everything is out of our control. And sometimes, it's just a bit of acknowledgment or encouragement that could mean all the difference.

That's what I learned over the course of my life, and that's what I try to give all my patients. People aren't always what they seem. Beneath every tough exterior is a soft heart. Most people just need a chance to let it show.

My exact set of circumstances has informed me the most on my journey as a nurse. Change one thing, and I can't say for certain that I'd be the same nurse and person I am today. And it makes sense. The curriculum was the same for me as it was for every other graduate of the nursing programs I completed over the years. But just because you've got the information doesn't mean you'll be good at the job. And likely, if you refer to it as a job, then you're probably not the best nurse on the floor.

So, what was it about my life that prepared me so well for this particular path?

I'm sure there are many others who have had experiences that resemble my own. But it was some combination of my closest influences and what I took away from my adversities that lit up a special compassion within me. Things will happen to all of us, that which we don't have much control, but it's how we handle the things that get thrown at us that most accurately predict the trajectory of our lives.

When I was born, my father was already the man he would always be. My home was waiting for me in the poor section of Long Island, New York. And I had genes and chromosomes in me already that would mean I'd grow up to be "thick and fine" in a world that prefers pencil thin.

But my mom was not a believer that we are a victim of circumstance, and she worked hard to make sure that we were not a product of our environment. And that was probably my earliest lesson. We went to church every Sunday, and she worked hard to provide for us. She spent most of her life as a certified nursing assistant (CNA), not attempting to go back to school to become a Licensed Practical Nurse until my sisters, brother and I were out of school. She put us first from day one.

Surrounding me were some great women. My grandmother was the ultimate encourager. She ingrained in me early on that I could be anything I wanted. Then there was my mother, who right up until her last breath was the most supportive presence in my life and a true hero to me. And last but not least, there was my Aunt, who worked as a nurse during her short life, but was taken from us too soon to accomplish her dreams in healthcare. For as long as I can remember, it's always been my dream to finish the mission of helping people that she didn't get a chance to help.

I'm the oldest of five siblings. My father left us when my mom was pregnant with my twin sisters, who are seven years younger than me. So, at the age of seven, I watched my dad not only go off with another woman but go off to play father to another child. This blew my mind. I couldn't understand how he could play the father role to a child that wasn't even his, especially when he had my soon-to-be sisters and me waiting for him at home. This seed of disappointment was planted early and grew through the years. For most of my life, my father has disappointed me, and this initial rejection was the start of that cycle.

It's funny the things we remember about our childhood. I remember spending summers with my dad's family. I'm not sure why, but whenever I was there, I suffered constant physical abuse and received whoopings for no reason. I could simply drink my juice too fast or eat my watermelon down to the rind, and I'd find myself getting spanked. It was physically painful, but it also hurt my spirit because I couldn't understand what I was doing wrong. Finally, I broke down and told my mother about it, and that ended my summer visits to Alabama.

But things didn't get better, though it wasn't until high school that I remembered this next part. It's interesting how we end up burying the things that hurt us. My mom had a close friend with a son about my age. I stayed with them while my mom was at work. The friend's husband was the one to watch us, and he was not a very wholesome man. I didn't realize at the time what exactly he was doing but later recalled that he was touching himself in front of me. He would even ask me to touch him with my hand. I don't think I completely understood what was going on, but I did know enough to know that it wasn't right. Eventually, I came to my breaking point; I started crying and said, "You're trying to make me do something that I don't want to do." That's the last I remember of the situation. For whatever reason, he no longer watched me after that, whether directly because of my outburst or for some other reason. But I suppressed this memory and didn't unearth it or tell my mother about it until I was in high school.

I believe the memory only came back at all because it was triggered by another similar event. My mother remarried my stepfather when I was around eleven. My stepfather had a nephew that came to visit us when I was in high school. The nephew was in his early twenties.

I remember him being friendly and generally amicable. But one night, I was sleeping in our shared room and woke up to find him stroking my back. He was muttering, "- I won't make you do anything you do not want to do." I wasn't sure how to react, so I feigned sleep while I tried to think of what next to do. Then, out of nowhere, the phone rang in the living room. My parents woke up to answer it, and he ran out. I ran out of the room as well and directly to my mom and told her what happened. Her initial reaction was shock, but she gathered herself quickly and told my stepfather. He immediately kicked his nephew out.

Though the threat was gone, and I understood that what happened wasn't my fault, I couldn't shake the feeling that there was something about me that was bringing these sorts of situations on. Why did people act this way around me?

When I got to high school, life was better. I was smart and in the top 5% of my class. I was class president, and on the surface, I seemed confident and strong. But under the surface, I still had a lot of insecurity and abandonment issues that probably stemmed a little from my past experiences and a lot from my absent father. It would take years before I was able to forgive him for all the abandonment I felt at his hands.

So, when I got to college, I was probably subconsciously looking to fill that void and find someone who could fulfill that need in me to be desired and loved. I was originally planning to go to Howard University but had to change my plans when I found out that my grandmother was sick. My stepdad and mom had moved to Florida; to be close to his mom; I would have to make a last-minute switch and go to Florida Agricultural and Mechanical University (FAMU) and pay out of state tuition. Because it was so last minute, I ended up living off campus and taking mostly night classes, to which I had to take public transportation. But the buses stopped at 5pm in Tallahassee, and there was no Uber back then, so I had to work extra hard to meet people who could drive me back and forth.

My first two semesters did not go well. I failed a couple of classes, stopped going to others; and got involved with a bad guy who got me pregnant, gave me a sexually transmitted disease (STD) and took off. In hindsight, I should've simply sat out the semester rather than starting off on such a rocky note, but at the time, I was adamant about going. Unfortunately, by the end, I had nothing but bad grades, an STD; and an abortion to show for it.

I believe that this profound event in my life is the reason that I am so passionate about teenage pregnancy prevention and safe sex. Young people think it can't happen to them, I share my story openly with my patients in hopes that they will listen and see the value of their life. We only have one life to live and it can be taken in an instance. I am an advocate of abstinence but if sexually active...cover it up, you can't always see an STD.

I remember feeling like I had reached rock bottom. I dropped out of school and moved back to New York to live with my grandmother. I felt like I had disappointed God, my mom and more importantly myself. When left to my own devices, I couldn't even stay focused on my dreams.

That summer, I was walking around with a ton of guilt. I didn't want to go back to school yet, so I took the semester off. That's when I met Darren, my now husband. Unlike the guy in college, Darren was a good guy. He supported me through the birth of our first child, Jaleesa, and going back to school to become a Licensed Practical Nurse (LPN). My first job as a nurse was at a nursing home; I remember wanting to work in a hospital, but they were not hiring LPNs at that time. Being limited to where I could work, and what I could do as a nurse did not sit well with me, so I started my quest to become a registered nurse. This mission eventually led me to Florida where my mom and stepdad lived. Although I took a huge pay cut to work at a Community Hospital in the small town of Palatka, it was worth it to be close to my family and to be able to work in a hospital setting.

The difference is like night and day going from a hospital in an urban area like New York to one in such a rural community. When I was in clinical, working on becoming an RN, the discrimination was palpable. I had a patient throw a full urinal at me, cursing at me to get out of his room because I was black. Wow, was my initial reaction followed by anger and then sadness. I had never experienced anything like that up north, but things were very different in the south.

Meanwhile, we were struggling to make ends meet, so my husband started driving trucks long distance. I can't say we didn't need the money at this point, but it left me feeling like a single parent because he was always on the road. At this point, I was raising two kids, going to school full-time and working full-time on the weekends.

As if I didn't have enough on my plate, I became pregnant with our third beautiful child. I had to stop school because it was a difficult pregnancy. I remember being so conflicted about withdrawing from the program. It felt like giving up, and like I was letting obstacles get in the way of my dreams. My Obstetrics instructor was one of those people who I felt was strategically placed by God in my life, and she assured me that I could just come back when I was ready; that they'd all be there when I got back. I couldn't help but feel like a failure, but her assurance gave me the kernel of hope that I needed. I thought to myself that's the type of instructor I would like to be one day.

Once Jada was born, I did go back. I finished school, graduated and officially became a Registered Nurse.

Again, being in such a rural area came with lots of opposition. I had learned early on from my mother not to be a victim of circumstances, but it was a struggle moving past such persistent opposition. It felt like everything I did, I had to work a little harder. I had to let more slide off my back. I had to be a little more optimistic. It was a fight to achieve every victory, like being the youngest charge nurse and the first black manager in my hospital.

But what really got me inspired was the lens through which I saw the world. I don't think I consciously made the connections every time I met a patient, but if I stop and think, I know that the accepting, loving manner I have with my patients is directly linked to what I craved and longed for growing up. Sometimes I found it, with my mother, my aunt or my grandmother, but sometimes I felt the void, the wish of something I couldn't quite articulate in my more difficult interactions.

One example stands out in my mind. There was a patient on our floor who was known to be difficult. He was made a quadriplegic from a gunshot wound, and he was difficult and curt with all of his nurses. On the day I was assigned to him, I came in like I always do, and introduced myself as his nurse. He responded, "Yes, you are today, and I'll probably have a new one tomorrow."

"Why do you say that?" I asked.

He responded, "No one wants to be bothered with me."

That's when it hit me. He wasn't talking about nurses at all. Well, maybe there was some truth to his statement, but the echo of a bigger issue came from a far deeper place. He felt extraneous and worth ignoring in his life.

It's actually not that far of a stretch from what I felt a lot of my life. I didn't feel ignored. I might've even wished people ignored me rather than abuse me. But being ignored and being mistreated are just two sides of the same coin - two different ways to NOT appreciate the person in front of you.

I knew what I needed to do. Sure enough, the next day, I was given a new assignment, which meant my patient would be given to a new nurse. I went to my manager and requested I stay with this patient. Then I walked into his room and said, "Good Morning Mr. Grumpy, my name is Dollicia and I'm going to be your nurse today." The smile that followed melted my heart. I not only heard his request, but I proved that his needs mattered enough that I came back.

Later that week, my manager came to me and asked what happened with Mr. Grumpy. After that day, he had stopped giving the nurses and certified nursing assistants (CNAs) a difficult time, and was now one of the best patients on the unit. I smiled at her, and simply said, "Sometimes people are not always what or whom they seem to be."

As much as a small moment can move you to appreciate others, a small moment can also make you appreciate yourself too. And no moment did this better than the time I saw myself in my patient. She could've easily been me. She was in her late 30s with a husband and four children at home. She went to the doctor that day with a strange headache and jaw pain, suspecting a bad tooth. It turned out to be an aneurysm, and she was now here in ICU undergoing brain surgery. What should have been an uncomplicated procedure, which I had seen so many times before, turned into a series of wrong turns. She never returned home.

I remember being overwhelmed by the thought that she left her home that morning just like any other day. Maybe she kissed her kids and said, "Mommy will see you later or I love you." Just like me, she was a mother, a daughter, a wife, a sister; and a friend, and just like that, she was gone.

This drove it home to me that there is no time to waste. I had taken many detours on my journey to becoming a nurse practitioner. But I knew now, more than ever, that I needed to make this happen, and more detours were not an option. Time is not always on our side, so there could be no more detours for me.

So, I did make it happen. The joy and pride in my mother's eyes as I walked across the stage to receive my master's degree in nursing is something I'll never forget. The year started off great. After graduation, I got my first nurse practitioner job, and I felt like I had finally arrived, and that this was what I was destined to do.

Through the years, I have helped many patients deal with the transition that comes with the loss of a loved one, but nothing could have prepared me for what was about to come.

On Christmas Eve 2016, my stepdad called me to come over because my mother wasn't acting right. She was sitting on the couch just staring. I thought she was having a stroke, so we called 911, and she was escorted to the hospital. When the results came back, things didn't look good.

She had brain cancer. There were four big lesions that they could see, and the scans showed multiple additional ones. Surgery was out of the question, and radiation would only prolong her life, not cure her. The news hit me like a bullet. My siblings and I, along with our stepfather never left her side. Christmas day was here, all the plans put on hold and I found myself praying to God with everything I had. I desperately pleaded with Him to bring her back to herself just long enough for me to really say goodbye.

Miraculously, I got my wish. Her mind came back, however fleetingly, for just a short time, but it was enough. She recognized us and was alert. We brought her home and did radiation at the hospice. As the nurse in the family, the responsibility fell to me to take care of her. I wished at the time that I could simply be her daughter, and prayed to God for strength.

Four days before my birthday and the day before Easter, she left us- and this earth - for good. But just before, she reached for my hand, and asked me a question she's asked a million times before. She said, "Are you going to be okay?" I answered, "Yes, Mom," and watched as a tiny tear escaped her eye and migrated down her cheek. She was always checking in on us right up until the very end, and once she was sure I'd be okay, only then was she okay with leaving.

That's when I felt reborn and became reacquainted with my life's purpose. I've always known that I wanted to follow in my aunt's footsteps in the healthcare industry, but I had forgotten how equipped my life made me for inspiring others in tough circumstances. I stopped noticing how all the struggles in my life led me to exactly where I am today. And I knew that I could help others similar to myself. My destiny is to help hurting women, especially, to show them that tons of bad things are going to happen. But it's not about blame or whose fault it is. It's not about judgment and shame. It's about staying the course, finding support and moving through it.

Faith has been the vehicle for me that has helped me through everything and that has been my support, and I encourage others to trust in God's plan. You're only given what you can handle. And the right people will be placed in your path, if you're open to receiving them.

I was born with a triad of strong women surrounding me, and every time I veered off course, God planted another supporter in my path. I was given many hardships, but I was also given an observant, loving and accepting nature, and I was able to use what I learned to help others. Today I am who I am because of my faith and because I trusted that my circumstances didn't define me. I was reminded through the passing of my mother, that I was actually given a lot when I came into this world – three women who helped define the core of who I am today, and a heart that was predisposed to love - - the heartbeat of a nurse.

Biography

Dollicia Green is a wife, mother, sister, friend and a highly respected Family Nurse Practitioner. She is passionate about the care she provides in her rural town.

Born to empower, inspire and motivate others, Dollicia has always had the heart for service. She is a nurse educator, community advocator and entrepreneur. She started her career in nursing as a Licensed Practical Nurse and is now pursuing her dream as a Board-Certified Nurse Practitioner. She is currently pursuing her Doctorate of Nursing Practice at the University of North Florida.

She began her nursing career at Putnam Community Medical Center after relocating from NY in 1996. At Putnam Community Medical Center, she held a variety of positions including staff nurse, charge nurse, interim nurse manager and assistant manager. Dollicia is self-motivated and loves to learn. She is always willing to share her knowledge, dreams and aspirations freely with others. She is committed to helping others reach their fullest potential. She is a servant leader, always modeling determination, strength, motivation, intelligence, and professionalism.

At UF Health in Gainesville, she continued her career as a staff nurse, intensive care nurse, charge nurse, mentor/preceptor, computer resource nurse and diabetes educator. Dollicia has over 20 years' experience in nursing and as a nurse practitioner she plans on continuing her impact to individuals on the preventative level and decreases hospitalizations of chronic illness by promoting regular checkups, disease management and preventative screenings.

She is also a certified legal nurse consultant and motivational speaker.

She is a member of The American Nurses Association (ANA), American Association of Nurse Practitioners (AANP) and the largest nursing association for black nurses, Black Nurses Rock. She is the President/CEO of the Gainesville Palatka Chapter. Dollicia is very familiar with the coordination and collaboration needed to host community service events and understands the needs of her local community. She is hands-on and loves to give back. She attends church at Abundant Life Ministries in Palatka Florida. She mentors middle school and high school girls on the importance of abstinence and safe sex.

Dollicia Green understands the importance of family. What she models in her profession and in the community, begins at home. She currently resides in Interlachen, Florida and she loves spending her leisure time traveling and helping others birth new visions. Dollicia's greatest passion is entrepreneurship. She is the Founder and CEO of a DIVA with a Truth, an inspirational platform, that motivates women in all aspects of life. This platform is yet another example of how she continuously pours into others. Deposits made into people's lives by Dollicia will have a legacy impact. #purposedtoimpact

Acknowledgement

I owe it all to my mother in law for inspiring me to become a nurse. I also will like to thank all my family and friends for supporting me, and a special thank you to RN Enterprise.

Sherita

We Have Something To Prove!

By Sherita Brown, RN, MBA

Growing up in Miami was not easy. I saw a lot of things and was also exposed to a lot at an early age. I was born in September of 1982. My father started calling me Chicken Little around the age of 10 and still does to this day. I have to remind him my name is Sherita Denise McCoy (Remember? This is what you and my mother named me!). Thinking back to when I was just a little girl, I've always had a passion for caring for others. It seemed to come naturally to me. From the young age of 4 yrs. old and, up until now, I have the same passion - possibly more so now than ever before. When I was younger, I always stated that I wanted to become a doctor. My parents married at an early age and had two kids: my brother and me. I also have a younger sister from my father. I learned, early on, how to nurture and protect my younger siblings. I would make sure that they ate and that they were taken care of - no matter what. If they got hurt, I was there to help them and make sure they were ok. Even though my parents were there to take care of them, I felt like I was their parent, too.

I remember the day my mother left my father. It was one of the worst times of me and my siblings' lives. We were severely affected by the separation and our lives changed forever. We started acting out. Our behavior changed and our grandparents had to step in. We ended up going to live with our fraternal grandparents. I would go between both grandparents' house, spending the weekdays with my father's parents and the weekends with my mother's parents. My brother would only go to my mother's parents' house sometimes. He would only go if we were going somewhere fun. We were blessed to have awesome, loving grandparents that were willing to step in and help raise us. My grandfather always worked hard to make sure that his family was taken care of. Don't get me wrong - our parents were still there and in our lives – but they also had a lot going on.

Meanwhile, living with my grandparents, I helped my grandmother take care of her aunt, who raised her. Being a little girl and seeing my grandmother taking care of her aunt helped me better understand caring for others and was important and meant a lot to my grandmother. I always wanted to be the helper and learn as much as I could by watching everything that she was doing to care for her aunt. I became my grandmothers' little helper and started helping with my great aunt, as well, while my grandparents went to work. I loved it because caring for others was something in which I took pride. My great aunt had Alzheimer's. Back then, we didn't have as much knowledge about Alzheimer's as we do now, but I did my best to care for my aunt. There were days when I would say to myself, "I am tired of taking care of her; I am a child," but there were also days I enjoyed putting a smile on my aunt's face because she felt like someone cared.

I mentioned earlier that I had a sister from my father. My little sister has alopecia. I've had to keep her lifted in my prayers and keep talking to her and let her know that she is beautiful no matter what - with or without hair. My sister is one of the strongest people I know; I never told her that when she was young. Looking back, we didn't have it easy growing up. I've experienced lots of bumps in the road to success and, in a sense, I'm glad that I did because all these bumps helped to mold me into the woman that I am today. Eventually, my father remarried and his new wife had a son and a daughter, so we gained two more siblings. We weren't happy that he had a new wife but it wasn't up to us. Gaining another brother and sister was a plus at first, but, after a while, I became upset because now I had another sister to take the attention off me. I was the oldest before my father remarried; once he remarried, my stepbrother was the oldest. Things were crazy, but I wouldn't change anything about it. Now I realize that everything happens for a reason. It only made me want to fight harder to be successful.

I finished high school on time and went on to a university that didn't really work out well. I dropped out of that school and started working full-time at Walmart and was able to get my own place. I met my husband while working at Walmart. I must say that my wedding day was one of the best days of my life! Marriage is not easy, but with prayer, compromise and working together, marriage is worth it. Soon after meeting my husband, I moved to Tampa and started school again to become an LPN. I didn't realize at that time I was on a path to what would be the best thing to happen to me. I was pregnant with my one and only girl. I didn't understand what it was to be a mother and how much work it really was until I became one.

I stopped school again because I was getting sick a lot during my pregnancy. After having my daughter, my mother became sick and passed away. I was lost and it took me awhile to get myself back together. I felt I could no longer go on without her. My baby brother ended up getting in trouble and had to go away to prison for a few years. At this point, I felt like I had nothing to lose. My mother was gone and so was my brother, but I pulled it together and told myself that it didn't matter to me, because I'm his big sister and I must be there for him no matter what. I wish it didn't happen, but it did. I really didn't want to go on, but I knew that I had to because I had a daughter who needed her mother. I finished LPN school in 2008 and I worked at the VA Hospital for a few years. That was a great experience - I could meet different people while doing what I loved. I gained knowledge and wisdom from the people I cared for and my co-workers.

Looking at my baby girl made me want to be a role model for her and keep pushing myself to be better. I then enrolled in RN school and became pregnant with my second child. History repeated itself: I didn't start school at the time I found out I was pregnant but, a year later, I decided to go back after my uncle said, "Sherita, you can do it! Go baby girl; you're almost there!"

However, right when I was about to get my RN degree, I was faced with another tragedy: my role model was ill. The only person who was always in my corner, and a call away, was in the hospital. This person was my uncle…but he was more than an uncle. He was my financial help when I needed him, he was the person that I looked up to and he was the one that I knew would always be there for me no matter what. So, I knew that I had to keep pushing and finish my RN degree. The day after finding out I passed my final exam to graduate, I was given the bad news by my husband - my uncle had passed away. My grandmother told my husband that she was unable to tell me because she knew I had been through so much. The three tragedies happened to me back to back. At this point, I was in a deep depression. With the power of prayer and encouraging words from my mother-in-law, I was able to defeat depression.

Now I was about to have my third and final child. I knew I wanted to be able to give my children the things that I didn't have growing up and the only way to do this was to keep bettering myself. I have had lots of long, stressful nights where I cried and cried and didn't know if I could do it. But I had my husband, who is my biggest supporter, right by my side and in my ear to keep pushing me to be the best that I can be. He pushed me to keep going to school and get my BSN degree and now I have my Master's degree. Right before graduating with my Master's degree, my family planned a trip to New York. However, it didn't feel quite right and I just knew something would go wrong. But I didn't say anything; I just prayed that I was wrong. And once again, I was faced with a tragedy. En route to New York, my Grandmother passed away on the plane. It felt like my heart was pulled out of my chest and there wasn't anything that I could do about it. The day that I got that call changed my life once again because it seemed that every time I reached a milestone in my life, I lost someone that meant a lot to me.

If that was not enough, I ended up in the hospital, a month after my grandmother's death, for shortness of breath, to only find out my goiter was growing inward, stopping the circulation of my windpipe. I had to have surgery to remove my thyroid with a month left of school to finish my Master's program. The surgeon stated what was supposed to be a 3-hour procedure turned into 5 hours. I am grateful to be here and given another chance. I feel as if I have something to prove. I believe that God has a purpose here for me and I will fulfill that purpose. Now, I'm in a great place in my life and feel that it's okay to take a small break before I go back to school to do my Doctorate degree. I don't know what or where I would be without my children, my husband, my family, my in-laws and my friends. I'm proud to say that I'm now in a better place - not only physically, but also spiritually - then ever before. I'm a role model to my children, my siblings, my husband, my friends and my family. I must say that I'm proud of myself, because I have been through so much and I'm sure others wouldn't have made it. But giving up wasn't for me. My brother is home and doing great and working hard. I'm so proud of the young man that he has become and can't wait to see all the great and wonderful things that he will do in the future. My little sister has grown up so much and she is now rocking her bald. I must say it looks great on her and I love it and her. She is BALD, BOLD and BEAUTIFUL! I'm also proud of her and glad that she's able to embrace who she is and love the skin she is in.

My husband has always had a heart of gold and he has shown me what real love is. He is my rock in every storm and he weather the storms with me. They say that a family that prays together stays together and I really believe that, because my husband made sure that we prayed and stayed in the LORD's house and it worked out for us. He is there for our three children and myself and gives us so much of him, effortlessly, and never looks for anything in return; I love him for that. When I was growing up, my family never set the table and had dinner together. However, in our house, we have family dinner as much as we can. At dinnertime, it's no phones or anything else - just family time. Our children are great kids -

they do well in school and they also play sports. Sometimes, it seems like we are always on the go and I don't know how we do it - but we make it work. I'm forever grateful and proud to call my husband MY HUSBAND, because without him, I wouldn't have this beautiful family and maybe wouldn't have worked so hard to better myself. I love coming home to my family and being a mother and a wife and hearing about their day and what they need and what they will be doing in the coming days. On those long nights when I'm so tired, I just think about them and the smiles they have on their faces and I'm reminded that I'm doing the right thing by them and that's all that matters.

I am now the proud owner of Our Loving Hands Companionship Services LLC. Our Facebook page is https://m.facebook.com/OLHCS. I am in the process of becoming a CEU provider and many more things to come. I enjoy what I do and I am determined to make sure quality care and services are provided to everyone. I look forward to working with many others and learning as much as I can to help others with success and health as well!! WE have something to prove!!!

Biography

Sherita Brown RN, BSN, MBA is the owner of Our Loving Hands Companionship Service LLC. Sherita has over 10 years of experience in Nursing. Her plan is to prevent hospitalization and help fulfill one of senior's biggest wishes, to remain at home. When she was young she was giving one of her biggest challenges in life. She was asked to help care for her aunt who raised her grandmother who was diagnosed with Alzheimer's. While everyone was at work and other kids were outside playing she was caring for her aunt. It was a challenge being a teenager caring for an adult with Alzheimer's but Sherita took pride in her job and did her absolute best. She did this for years until her aunt passed away. As you can see it's always been a passion of Sherita to take care of seniors and others. Sherita started out as a CNA, then moved to a LPN, and now practices as a RN with a Master's Degree in health care. Sherita has seen health care from many different views in Nursing over the years. She is now working on becoming a CE provider to help keep nurses updated on their skills and the revolving care of nursing. Sherita will also be collaborating with other Arthurs and publishing a book next year. Sherita enjoys being with family and friends and having a great time! She reads in her spare time to stay updated with new information. She is married with 3 kids whom she loves dearly.

Acknowledgements

I would like to express a special thanks to Michelle Rhodes for giving me the opportunity to be part of an amazing experience. It is because of your encouragement and mentorship that I am able to complete this project and begin on my personal book that God placed on my heart so long ago.

Secondly, I would also like to thank my family for always being there to support me in all my endeavors. It is very much appreciated. And a special thank you to my beautiful daughter Vontese McNeil who has been my rock through so much, I love you pumpkin. My best friend Rasaan Scales who never let me quit even when I wanted to.

Lastly, I would like to thank Aundretta Dickson, Marquita Stevenson, Joy Rembert and Shalonda Smith for the love, support, laughs and tears we shared during and after nursing school. And Mrs. Karen Ivers for being that teacher whom brought out the best in us.

I dedicate this book to Shalonda Smith; may you rest peacefully in paradise. You are truly missed and loved.

Deidre

Beating the Odds

By Deidre McNeil, BS LPN

I sit here, eyes closed, my mind overwhelmed with the reflections of God's great blessings through the journey of my life and how the storms we push through become our living testimony. This was not my chosen path, but one chosen by God and, through it all, I have found my heart's passion.

My name is Deidre McNeil, the third born of four siblings, and the forty-year-old mother of three beautiful children. I want to introduce you to how I found my passion and became a nurse. Through my journey, I have found that nursing is more than a career choice - it's a calling. If you don't have the passion for nursing, this is not the career for you, as it requires much. But the rewards are amazing! The positive feelings you get when you make a difference in the lives of those in need is endless. Nursing is filled with many emotions, but, through it all, you will be able to say, with confidence, that you have done all you could to make someone's roughest time better, or even someone's last days beautiful.

I can remember so many moments in my nursing career that made such an impact on me, good and bad. Don't get me wrong - there are many good times with fuzzy feelings - but there are some bad ones, too and on those bad days are the times where you must remember the "why" of what you do. Many girls and guys grow up with dreams of becoming doctors, nurses or other fantastic occupations that may spark the passion in them. But not all stay that path. For some, life happens, and they start to see their dreams as a distant memory or a task too hard to reach. I can remember back in nursing school how the classroom was filled with people of all different ages that expressed how becoming a nurse was their lifelong dream.

Well, for me, that was far from my dream. When I was younger, all I could see myself doing was becoming a licensed cosmetologist and I did just that. But as I stated earlier, God had other plans for my life, so after an accident, I found myself starting my journey through nursing school. Isn't it funny how God works? Anyhow, I loved to make people feel beautiful and we all know when a woman gets a new hairdo, or even a man with a new haircut/shape-up for that matter, it can make that person feel like a million bucks. That was my motto: when you look good, you feel good, and confidence is the key. So, as a single young mother, I followed my passion and became a licensed cosmetologist. But, in the end, it still felt like something was missing…even before the accident. I was not satisfied. One of the dreams I had was owning my own salon/spa so that the whole person could be pampered and refreshed. Self-care is so important to the mind and body.

Nursing gave me an even bigger platform to become an even bigger help for people as a healthcare professional.

I never thought of myself as a nurse but found that a lot of the women in my family were nurses. My grandmother was a nurse back in the 1960-70's, which introduced my mom into the nursing world. It took my mom eighteen years working as a certified nurse assistance to finally decide to pursue her career as an LPN. My mother's drive showed me that it is never too late to pursue your dream. After I completed nursing school my sister Jeanette started her journey following the family trend. My nursing journey began in 2002 and it was one of the most challenging journeys I've been on so far.

It was an amazing time in my life and I got to go on this journey with one of my closest friends/family, my sister-in-law, Dretta. I can remember back to the time after taking the NET entrance exam and going through the intensity of the interview, we were on pins and needles waiting to find out if we got accepted. We knew, just like those that have been through it, that if we received the little envelope it was a no-go, but if we received the large yellow envelope, it was time to give up our social life and brace ourselves for the life of a nursing student. Gratefully we were both accepted!

Nursing school was hard and the best advice I could give to anyone entering is to be organized, attend every class and stay on top of your work. Yes, you will most likely become a social misfit, because you will miss events and not have time to socialize, but I promise it is so worth it in the end. Nursing school was awesome, and I got to meet some amazing people that helped me grow, so that once I graduated, I could be ready. Throughout school, I saw students have mental breakdowns, panic attacks - all due to the hard dedication it takes to maintain the life of a nursing student.

Whenever times got hard and I felt like throwing in the towel, I would just think back to why I wanted to become a nurse in the first place. Quitting was not an option, and neither was failure, so no matter what I learned, to have my moment and then pull myself together so that I could have victory in the end was so well worth it. The overwhelming joy you feel when you know you have won that battle is incredible. So many students began with us, but only a few made it. Not too scare anyone, but just like I have told others in the past after much encouragement, go for your dream in pursuing your nursing career - just know that it is not an easy road but a very rewarding one.

Nothing compares to that accomplishment of completion. In our nursing school, the passing grade percentage was 78%, so whenever our grades were posted, we would race to the wall to see if we made it. Talk about anxiety! There were sighs of relief when you knew you made it through the hurdles, and were that much closer to the finish line. There was one instructor in our school that we all were scared of or intimidated by because we knew when we came to her, we better have it together. I mean, we had to make sure our T's were crossed and out I's were dotted because she would surely test your knowledge. In the end, this is the instructor that had the largest impact on my career, because she taught me so much and made me think and work harder. She also taught us to stand up for ourselves in the field because we are the ones that fought so hard to obtain our licenses. Mrs. Ivers was one of the best instructors I had and, to this day, what I've learned from her is implanted in my brain.

As I sit here writing this the memory of my first nursing job, it comes back to me like it was yesterday. 5:30 am in the morning. Waking up and getting myself prepared to put all the things I've learned into my new career as a Licensed Practical Nurse. I cannot tell you the mixed emotions that exploded inside of me. I was a bag of nerves, scared that I would not be able to do the job…but there was no turning back. Every new nurse experiences these feelings; it is extremely rare for a new nurse to enter their first job with 100% confidence and no fear. Fear is that too familiar feeling to all but the ones who accomplish the task without letting it keep them from feeling truly victorious. One of the best quotes I've heard is, "Do is scared," because that means to never quit. When we let fear keep us from doing the things that we want, we cheat ourselves. We let the fear of "what if?" play with our minds. But my question to that is, "But what if it does work out?" Well, on this day, fear had to disappear, because quitting was not an option. I believe that nursing is a calling and not just a career, so most have a passion to care for others, advocate for their patients and be the voice when their patients cannot be. Nursing is a powerful calling and I would advise anyone going into it to believe in yourself and never let anyone detour you from the path God has placed you on. I have encountered older nurses that were awesome and willing to take me under their wing until I could fly on my own. And then there are those nurses that are said to "eat their young."

My first job was working in a long-term care nursing facility and I decided to start at one with the worse reputation, because I figured that would make all the others easier - and it did. This facility was filled with patients that other facilities wouldn't accept, and a lot were even abandoned by their loved ones. Well, the Director of Nursing at this facility was a young African American woman that had graduated from my school years prior, so it was good to see her in that position - until I got to know more about her work manner. This woman would curse at and demean her staff and was totally unprofessional. She was an example of how not to act when you are placed in a position of leadership. True leadership is being an example to staff and displaying professionalism with respect for people. We have all started somewhere and can quickly lose everything if we decide to behave in such unethical and unprofessional ways. All experiences, good and bad, can work out to your benefit. Some show you what not to do and others encourage you to strive for the best you that you can be. I learned so much on my journey as a nurse and continue to learn today. Nursing is a profession in which learning is continuous, and those in the field should be open to that continuous learning. No nurse - no matter how many years - will know everything, but just about every nurse has something to offer to another nurse.

I can remember one experience that I could have felt offended but found it funny instead. Yes, this is also a field in which you must have a sense of humor, too. Otherwise, things can make you step out of your character and that is not what you want to do. I believe I was in the 3rd year of my nursing career and working for an agency assigned to a well-known long-term care facility. I walked on the unit and over to the nurses' station to see which nurse I would be relieving. The nursing station was filled; the usual change of shift hustling going on, with nurses trying to finish up, so they could leave, and the CNAs filling out their last bit of paperwork along with those coming on to get report. Well, I walked over, and this one older Caucasian nurse asked if I was working on the unit that day. I replied, "yes." Immediately, she turned to the CNA and called out the number that would be working this evening, which included me. I stood there and sort of chuckled to myself when the other Caucasian nurse walked up to see who was her relief staff. Oh, did I mention that most of the nurses were Caucasian and most of the CNA's were African American? Well, yes. So, I guess they just assumed that this little black girl could not be the nurse. I kindly stated, "That would be me" and looked at the Caucasian nurse, whose face was now red. I handed her back the CNA assignment she had just given me as I made my way into the medication room for report. Let's just say she was dumbfounded but never even uttered an apology for her assumption. Now I can say I was a little offended because I believe she took one look at me and assumed that I could not have been the nurse, instead of asking me anything, But, as the saying goes, when you assume you make an ass out of you and me. Yes, this was an older Caucasian nurse whom I would have a few more incidents with over the four years I worked at this facility. As a nurse in this field, especially an African American nurse, I had to have tough skin because of so many racially ignorant people with whom I worked or encountered. But I also got the chance to work with some awesome nurses of all races and backgrounds from whom I learned and developed great friendships, and for that I am grateful.

I love being a nurse, even with the long hours and craziness of it all. The world of nursing is open to so many opportunities in many different areas. Over the years, I have worked in various settings, from a community clinic to a psychiatric correctional facility. This is where I found my love for mental health and pursued my bachelor's degree in Psychology, which I obtained in 2013 from the University of Bridgeport. I became a nurse case manager for the special needs program, which gave me a way to utilize my love for nursing and psychology. We all must find the area to which our passion drives us, and it may not be the one you always thought it would be. In the beginning, I thought labor and delivery would be the area in which I worked, due to my love for babies and the beauty of pregnancy, but during our clinical rotation, that quickly changed. There was a young pregnant female who had to deliver her baby that was stillborn, and she was totally heartbroken (as to be expected). Watching her, and knowing that what she was going through had to be one of the worst experiences of her life, was difficult. In school, we were always told that we needed to show empathy and try not to get emotionally attached, but this was a hard one for me, so I was broken, too much so to work in that environment, so I found out that was not my area. Just because the area of nursing is not where you find your calling to be does not mean that nursing is not for you.

In life alone, we encounter so many obstacles placed in front of us, and when you go into a profession like nursing, as an African American, the obstacles are even greater. As much as I hate that the world is this way, this is the reality of the environment - even in a profession that should be filled with love, compassion and caring. We must be the change we want to see, but at the same time, stand up against those who believe they can treat us as less. Today, I continue my journey to go further in my nursing career, which is taking longer than I thought or wanted, but life sometimes does that. My experiences have made me more determined to complete my goals and, along the way, I have had the pleasure of meeting and connecting to those that motivated me even more. It does make things harder when you have mothering responsibilities, but nothing worth having is going to be easy; there are always sacrifices. Having family support is huge when it comes to reaching a goal that requires so much of your time, energy and focus. I have witnessed nursing students that did not have this support and lost marriages and relationships in the process. I believe that this is a breakdown in communication, because when a person decides to enter nursing school, it should be discussed that their attention will have to be on completing their program.

As I stated before, it is a sacrifice and the end can be better for all those involved in supporting their loved ones during their journey.

One very important fact that I have learned is that the person on this journey will never be more than you believe yourself to be. You need to be your biggest cheerleader. God put vision in me that I will fight to see come to pass, no matter what age I am or when I complete it. There are many times I have failed and let the spirit of procrastination stop me from moving towards my goals, but when that happens, I must pull myself together and just do it. Life is too short to waste time, so I must motivate myself to keep pushing through.

Currently I am working on obtaining my associates degree and even though it has taken some time, I can see the light at the end of the tunnel. During our life, we are filled with so many decisions on whether we should go further in our career and wonder if we have what it takes to pursue our dreams. My advice is that no matter whom you may encounter during your journey - whether it be nursing school or even in the nursing field - never let someone take you down, because this is your journey and people may try to stop you from living out your purpose. Be confident, be courageous, be fearless and be your biggest cheerleader. It took me years to realize that you may not get the encouragement from others that you feel you need; instead, you need to encourage yourself. There is no greater feeling than when you reach the point of completion of your goals; making small goals and continuously achieving them, one by one, to reach the ultimate one you may have thought was why out of reach. Celebrate all your achievements because you did it. Be victorious because you are awesome!

Biography

Deidre McNeil is an author, nurse and mother of three beautiful children residing in North Carolina, born in Bridgeport Connecticut. She is a Licensed Practical Nurse with a Bachelors degree in Psychology obtained from the University of Bridgeport and continues to pursue her passion.

Acknowledgements

I am honored and grateful for the opportunity to share my story in hopes to inspire, uplift and empower women around the world. I believe helping others through educating is my earthly assignment.

First, I would like to thank God for molding me into the woman I am today. Thank you for placing in me a fearless, resilient and empowering spirit. I truly am nothing without you. Because of you Lord, I live boldly and confident.

To my family, especially my husband Wade Buggs, I am truly blessed to have you in my life. You definitely were the glue that held our family together during my military career. Thank you for believing in me, encouraging me and loving me unconditionally. I love you forever. Whitney, Imani and Wade, I know at times I can be a thorn in your side but it's only to make you all better. I hope that this story will encourage you to move forward when you are faced with challenges and failures throughout your lifetime. I love you all dearly. To my parents, thank you for your unconditional love towards me. You both have been an outstanding support system to Wade and I and we can't thank you enough. I love you both. To all my friends, thank you for your continuous support in all that I do.

To Michelle Rhodes, thank you for presenting this opportunity to me. You are truly an inspiration to many and I am so glad God placed you in my path. I pray that God will continue to bless you tremendously.

Victoria

The Good, the Bad, the Victory: Threefold Reflections

By Victoria Y. Buggs, MPH, RN

For I know the plans I have for you, declared the LORD, plans for good and not for evil, to give you a future and a hope. Jeremiah 29:11

Ever since I was a little girl, I've been outgoing, outspoken, and adventurous. In elementary school, I was the kid who participated in all the school events from spelling bees to fashion shows and talent shows. I was chosen to recite "Mother to Son," by Langston Hughes, at the citywide Black History event. I even sung "Greatest Love of all," by Whitney Houston, at my sixth-grade graduation. Boy, did I sound awful! But I finished strong with confidence and conviction. Throughout my primary years of education my mom would ask me why I carried so many books? Where is your book bag? At an early age, I became attracted to learning and teaching others to learn. Reading and writing were my all time favorite subjects in elementary and middle school. It was not until I attended high school that I found my true love, purpose, and my being. I became a member of the Junior Reserve Officer Training Corps (JROTC). JROTC is a military regulated high school program whose purpose is to educate high school students in leadership roles while making them aware of the benefits of citizenship.

I spent four years in JROTC. During my junior year, I became the Co-captain of the unarmed female drill team and during my senior year, I was the Captain of the unarmed drill team. During that time, my high school received second place in the citywide unarmed drill team competition. After being successful in twice leading a group of young ladies to victory, my self-confidence, self-esteem, and self-worth began to increase. I went to every JROTC camp the high school offered. During each course, I learned the fundamentals of leadership, mental toughness, integrity and selfless service. At age 18, I began to illustrate the behaviors and characteristics of a leader. These attributes included passion, motivation, self-belief, hard work, discipline and dedication. As a child growing up, we never know what or whom we wanted to be when we grow up. However, after the extensive training I received and leadership opportunities that the JROTC offered to me, it was then I knew I wanted to serve my country and become a leader. I wanted to serve in the military once I graduated high school.

On May 15, 1995, I enlisted into the United States Army as a Private First Class. Shortly after my high school graduation June 5,1995, I attended basic training in Fort Leonard Wood, Missouri, for 6 weeks and advance initial training for 5 weeks in Fort Jackson, South Carolina.

Sky is the Limit...

In August of 1999, I was offered an opportunity to reenlist and attend college fulltime for a semester at my college of choice. During this time, I did not know in what I wanted to enroll, so I did some research and decided I wanted to explore becoming a Medical Assistant. I spent 6 months doing the basic courses, which were required prior to moving on to the core courses. Coming from a family of nurses, I mentioned that I was going to school to become a medical assistant and the first question was "why not nursing?" My aunt had been a nurse for almost 20 years and was working on her Masters in Nursing when she convinced me that nursing was the more rewarding profession.

During the next semester, I changed my major and registered for nursing at the local community college. Due to my military schedule, I was unable to attend fulltime, so I went during the night for all my science and prerequisite courses. In 2004, I finally graduated from Anne Arundel Community College with an Associate's degree in General Studies not nursing. Due to the scheduling conflict of clinicals in nursing, I had to postpone my dreams of becoming a nurse. Because I loved everything about educating patients, health promotion and disease prevention, I knew it was only a matter of time before I would be back studying nursing.

During my time as a student I learned adaptability, emotional stability, quick responsiveness, flexibility and respect. These attributes were needed as I pursued my Bachelors Degree in Health Science, Health Educator. My curriculum included Health Promotion and Disease Prevention, Environmental Health and Safety and my favorite course; Principles of Teaching/Clients and Groups along with a host of other courses that I credit to my success today. Because of these characteristics of passion, motivation, self-belief, hardwork, discipline and dedication, I was able to complete my degree and graduate Magna Cum Laude (GPA 3.785) all while being deployed to Iraq OIF 2006-2007.

During my deployment, I worked at medical facility, where I served as the Casualty Liaison, Non-Commissioned Officer In Charge. My duties included reacting to mass casualty calls, reporting medical accidents and scheduling medical evacuation flights to higher level medical facilities within the area of operation and assisting in routine and severe medical emergencies. What a great fit for me as I felt I was being groomed for my passion. However, with that experience came lots of heartache and sleepless nights. Visions of missing body parts, screams, and visits to the mortuary replayed over and over in my mind. "Am I built for this?" I questioned myself.

Prior to deploying to Iraq, I applied for a prestigious program called the Army Enlisted Commissioning Program. The AMEDD Enlisted Commissioning Program (AECP) provides eligible Active Duty, Reserve, National Guard, or AGR ARMY SOLDIER's the opportunity to complete a Bachelor of Science in Nursing (BSN) and receive a commission in the Active Duty component of the ARMY Nurse Corps. The requirement is to be able to obtain a Bachelor's Degree in Nursing with 24 months while maintaining a 3.00 or above. Additionally, you could pick your school of choice and the program was fully funded for each participant. If selected, I would finally receive a second chance at pursuing a career in nursing.

The Good Life...

"Have I not commanded you? Be strong and courageous. Do not be afraid; do not be discouraged, for the LORD your God will be with you wherever you go." Joshua 1:9

Round of applause; I got accepted into the Army Enlisted Commissioning Program! I was also accepted into Howard University's Division of Nursing Program. Life is good. Soon, I will be pursing my dreams as a nurse and utilizing my new skills as I become a nursing professional. Definitely a dream come true and I was ready to embrace the challenge.

However, I was faced with my first wave of adversity. The unit I was supporting while deployed was not so happy for me. The senior leadership wanted me to defer my future dreams in becoming a nurse and continue to lead my Soldiers. It was a huge dilemma however, my Soldiers cheered me on and let me know through their actions they could handle the deployment without me. I requested a 90-day advance release, but it was disapproved. I literally fought to get released three weeks prior to the semester starting. Never give up on your dreams.

During my two academic years at Howard University, the nursing staff diligently drilled in us the importance of being competent, caring and passionate nurses. I was a very conscientious nursing student. I was always asking questions to get a better understanding of the nursing processes and disease processes. I wanted to ensure I provided my patients with correct answers within my scope of practice.

Every week, I could not wait to get to clinical. The excitement of getting my patient assignment was so surreal. My favorite clinical rotations were Medical-Surgical, Maternity, Community Health, Leadership and Psych. Living in the Washington D.C. Metropolitan Area, I had the opportunity to work with numerous experienced nurses and do clinical work at some great hospitals. I was doing a psych rotation at Howard University Hospital where the late Mayor Marion Barry was having his liver transplant surgery. The experiences and opportunities of learning were unmatched, and I am forever grateful for the opportunity.

As I reflect on my nursing experience as a student, I realize that I was being molded to become much more than a nurse. The more I interacted with a patient, did a group project, or a class presentation, the more my desire to educate increased. I became more empathetic, compassionate and personable. My passion for the profession and my patients kept me focused as I knew that I was developing into something greater than just a leader and nurse.

Not only did I strive to become a better nurse, but I also met a group of student nurses who pushed me to be better. We all studied hard to ensure the group was successful. Several of my study buddies were also selected to a program similar to AECP but it was through the U.S. Navy. Another study buddy was a military veteran, her contributions to the group were exceptional. She was very thorough and meticulous when it came teaching concepts and skills.

Throughout my academic career, I was often called upon to teach my fellow colleagues how to perform a procedure, assist in a study group, or participate in a weekend project educating the community or attending a seminar. I recall being a Stroke Ambassador via the American Heart Association. I must admit through all the chaos at the Howard University Division of Nursing, my leadership skills and nursing attributes were beginning to create a new and better nurse once I began to use them together. I was open-minded about the numerous opportunities in nursing and could not wait to explore which would be best for me once I graduated and passed my **National Council Licensure Examination** (NCLEX).

As the time drew closer to take my NCLEX, I began to dream about all the patients I would nurse back to good health. I could see myself as a nurse educator, helping the masses. I even had moments where I thought I would open a nonprofit organization to help those who did not have health insurance, access to health care or medication. I was ready to save the world. Victoria Y. Buggs, RN, BSN, super nurse and healthcare extraordinaire.

This is Bad…Failure

And let us not grow weary of doing good, for in due season we will reap, if we do not give up. Galatians 6:9

After graduation, it was time to find a NCLEX review course. As a group we decided to go with ATI. The course length was 5 days. Upon completion of the course, I studied 4 hours a day and answered 100 NCLEX questions for 30 days in preparation for the NCLEX. When the day finally came, I was full of anxiety. I could hardly think. I sat to take the test and it seemed as if it was the longest day ever. Mentally, I was pooped. I remember heading home and talking to my husband with no voice. I was so scared that I did not pass. Forty-eight hours later, I looked on the Maryland Board of Nursing website to see that I was not a nurse and I failed the NCLEX.

I was so disappointed. How could I fail something for which I thought I had prepared? I questioned myself for about a week. I hid myself in my study room and isolated myself from anything and everything but studying. I refused to be defeated and vowed to go back and beat the NCLEX. I contacted ATI to let them know that I was unsuccessful in passing the NCLEX. They partnered me up with a tutor. I had assignments every day. I was passing every assignment, quiz and test they gave me. I was notified by my tutor I was ready to retest.

Take two…testing day! I was ready, my confidence was back, and defeat and failure were not an option this go around. The first time I took the test, I had 265 questions and it took me 6 hours to complete. This time, I only had 125 questions and about 3 ½ hours before completion. Wow, I was super nervous and it stopped way too fast this time. I was so scared; I couldn't talk… but I felt better. The questions all seemed familiar I could even remember some of the questions this time.

It had been 48 hours now and I needed to check to see if I was the nurse I had been patiently waiting to be. Oh, my goodness… I failed AGAIN. I'm a two-time NCLEX failure. I was so devastated.

I truly wanted to die right then and there. My self-esteem had hit rock bottom. I needed to compose myself fast because I had to notify the AMEDD point of contact that I failed again. It was so hard to say that I failed at something which I had worked so hard. I put on my big girl panties and made the call. I was informed that I will be disenrolled in becoming an Army Nurse and sent back to Active Duty Army as an enlisted member. It was a hard pill to swallow, not just for me, but for my family as well. Let me share with you what I learned from my failures:

1. The sweetest victory is the most difficult one.

2. Continue to persevere and don't give up.

3. In difficult moments seek God just as in good moments and in every moment thank God.

4. Embracing failure is how you grow and learn.

5. Learn from your failures to become successful.

Victory is Mine…

"All things are possible to those who Believe" Mark 9:23

Now that I have gotten my mind right, it was time to go back to the lab and get this nursing license that I worked so hard to achieve. Howard University was having an event and I decided attend and see some old friends and hear the successes of my colleagues and thinking maybe they could assist me in passing the NCLEX the third time around. I saw so many people and I discussed my failures with them and they offered so many kind words and reminded me why I deserved my nursing license and encouraged me to not give up. I also ran into my Medical Surgical teacher. We talked about my failures and she told me that I had test anxiety. She offered up this advice "Know what you know and know it well."

I took it to heart! This teacher often told me that I would make a great nurse and the nursing profession needed me. I felt as if so many people were depending on me and I was letting them down. I used all advice and test taking techniques offered to reduce my anxiety. I reduced my study time to two hours a day for theory, one-hour questions and one-hour test taking techniques. I felt my positivity coming back. I began to feel empowered and most of all confident. I was back. I prayed, gave myself a pep talk and put it in God's hands.

December 7, 2009, I got dressed in my business attire; my hair was done from the weekend and I put on some make up and headed to the testing site. I was feeling great and inspired. I left my home knowing that I would be victorious this time. I also knew if things didn't go my way, I had nothing to lose. I was already heading back to the big Army anyway, so it didn't matter. It was show time.

I was sitting at the computer and question #1 was on the screen it was easy. On to the next question. I began to use the techniques that I learned through my 45 days of studying. I utilized the white board to write out what I knew and compared it to the answers that were on the screen. If I had it on my board and it was on the screen, it was the correct answer. This technique worked, and I looked up and the screen stated I was done; less than 100 questions.

I was done! I was so numb. I rested my head on the desk and prayed. I closed out what was on the screen, got up and exited the room. I left the building feeling blah but hopeful. I called my husband to tell him that I finished the test, but again no voice. Anxiety wins.

On December 9, 2009, my husband woke me up early in the morning and summoned me downstairs. He was very desperate and angry about the computer screen. I didn't know what happened. He told me to look at the crack in the computer monitor but I was still asleep and could not see. He pointed to the screen upon which the back ground words stated I was an active nurse. There was no crack in the screen. He looked up the results for me and was the first to notify me that I had succeeded. I was a finally a registered nurse and he was a proud husband.

There's Victory in Failing

The latter glory of this house will be greater than the former,' says the LORD of hosts, 'and in this place I will give peace,' declares the LORD of hosts." Haggai 2:9

Now it's time for me to head back into the big Army. I was so disappointed, but God does not make any mistakes. This time I had to relocate to Fort Bragg, NC where I deployed for one year. Meanwhile, I reapplied to the AMEDD department to become a commissioned officer in the Army Nurse Corp. In April 2011, I completed my Master's Degree in Public Health with honors while deployed. Prior to redeployment, I was notified I was selected for a position at William Beaumont Army Medical Facility in Fort Bliss,

Texas as an Army Nurse with a $40,000 bonus upon my return. Sound great right? Unfortunately, I declined this fantastic opportunity due to the length of the Basic Officer Leadership Course, the relocation of my family and my daughter being in her senior year of high school. The stability of my family was most important to me at that time.

After returning to Fort Bragg, I began moonlighting at Womack Army Medical Center telemetry floor to hone my nursing skills. Later I was assigned to the Defense Threat Reduction Agency, where I met a woman who educated me on becoming my own boss. She inspired me to become an entrepreneur. The first thing that came to mind was to start a business that utilized my ability to lead, educate, and inspire coupled with my higher education.

I attended Veteran Women Igniting the Spirit of Entrepreneurship (V-Wise). V-WISE is a premier training program in entrepreneurship and small business management. V-WISE helps women veterans and female military spouses/partners find their passion and learn the business savvy skills necessary to turn an idea or start-up into a growing venture. The three-phases of the program include a 15-day online course (Phase I), 3-day entrepreneurship training event (Phase II) and ongoing mentorship, training and support opportunities for graduates launching or growing their businesses (Phase III).

I was so inspired and empowered that shortly afterwards, I obtained my certification as a CPR instructor and registered to become an approved training center for the American Safety and

Health Institute (ASHI). Secondly, I attended Project Opportunity, another entrepreneur course that assisted veterans in becoming entrepreneurs and small business owners. Project Opportunity is a 10-week program that offers training, outreach services, technical assistance and financing opportunities to veterans considering starting a business. Both courses prepared me to step out on faith and launch my business Center for Health Educators and Safety Specialists, LLC.

There is no appropriate time to start a business. Passion and drive is all you need to start. So, start when you get the urge. I mentioned earlier how I was being developed to be a great leader, nurse and now entrepreneur. Each attribute of a leader, nurse and entrepreneur complement each other. The more my passion to become an entrepreneur grew, the hungrier I became for knowledge. I feed by hunger by learning more about my business and companies I would collaborate with and provide my services too.

As I reflect back on my journey, I realized that I was never prepared for the battle until I failed. It was with failure that I found humility and resilience. Through perseverance and determination is where I found my true strength. Knock down after knock down reminded me that true success was getting up and starting over again. But thanks be to God, who always leads us in triumph in Christ, and manifests through us the sweet aroma of the knowledge of Him in every place, Corinthians 2:14, KJV. As I move forward with my business venture, I am prepared to face failure with an open mind. You too will face many failures or challenges in your life but don't give up; stay encouraged.

It has been a joy to let you in on one of my most painful experiences of my life. I leave with you to always remain relevant, intentional and purposeful in everything that you do. Seek as much knowledge as you can in the field in which interest you. Network like crazy and find a coach or mentor! Surround yourself with like-minded people. Always pray and stay humble. Offer advice to others and ask for help. Someone is waiting for you to come along. Believe me they need you as much as you need them! Thank God for all the opportunities in advance because you never know which one will change your life forever. Educate, Empower and Elevate...

Biography

Victoria Y. Buggs was born and raised in Gary, Indiana. She resides in Severn, MD. She is a 20-year disabled combat veteran who retired at the rank of Sergeant First Class from the United States Army. Her nursing career started in August 2007 as a nursing student at Howard University, where she obtained her Bachelors of Science Nursing degree. Prior to nursing school, Victoria had obtained a Bachelors of Science Health Science degree as a Health Educator, from Tourou International University. Magna Cum Laude was awarded to her for academic success. While on numerous deployments her passion for healthcare did not stop. She volunteered to work at the 506 eMEDs while serving as a Casualty Liaison, Non-Commissioned Officer in charge. There she assisted in the daily operations of providing healthcare to wounded service members and scheduling transportation to higher level medical facilities within the area of operations. Throughout her busy deployments she found time to complete her Master's degree in Public Health from Trident University. Upon arriving stateside, Victoria began moonlighting at Womack Army Medical Facility on an outpatient telemetry unit. From their she secured a job at BonSecour Hospital working in telemetry, West Baltimore. Because she is no stranger to providing training, evaluating training programs, writing training plans and curriculum she decided to step out on faith and start a small business. In 2015, Victoria launched Center for Health Educators and Safety Specialists, LLC, where she is working part time. Center for Health Educators and Safety Specialists, LLC, currently provides CPR services and safety training to healthcare professionals and laypersons. Her goal is to work full time, and be a fully operational, one stop shop training center, through obtaining local, state, and federal contracts. Victoria has obtained her Woman Owned Small Business certification and Department of Veteran Affairs verified Service Disabled Veteran Owned Small Business Certification. In 2017, Victoria was awarded the Maryland Hero Award at the Maryland Military & Veteran Woman Business Conference.

To Contact the Author:

Phone: 410-834-1528

Email: ctr4hess@gmail.com

FB: https://m.facebook.com/C4HESS

Victoria Y. Buggs
MPH, RN, BSN

Acknowledgements

I am forever grateful to God for His continual love, support, and dedication to me. I am thankful for the vision to create something that will help others be successful as I have been.

I would like to dedicate this book to my parents and my brother who have supported my career and visions from day one.

And lastly, to each person that has touched my life in some form throughout the years,

I say thank you.

"My goal is that each reader will find peace and healing in the mist of your storms, the strength to forgive others including yourself, the ability unpack the bags of doubt and insecurity and the desire to actively operate in your God-driven purpose."

Alvionna

TRANSPARENCY
Claiming Victory in Life and in Nursing

By Alvionna Brewster, BSN, RN

I am broken pieces. The depths of my soul have been crushed and crumbled over and over again. Some partly due to my own fault. Some…not.

My breaking point came in 2012. I was dating a gentleman who was significantly older than myself. Against my better judgement, I gave in to his charm and persistence. Offers to treat me like a queen and even threats of marriage had me childishly smitten. The first few months were typical. Butterflies, intimate dates, quiet evenings and little sweet gifts. But a few months in, I started noticing odd behaviors. Random outbursts of anger and small remarks of belittlement were becoming the norm. These actions were always smoothed over with "At least I'm not like your last boyfriend or you are just immature, you need to grow up."

During this season, I was in nursing school for a second time, working a job that I hated, in this terrible relationship, suffering from illness, and dealing with the death of my two grandparents. The weight of the world trampled my spirit. I was merely a skeleton drifting through life.

The ultimate betrayal came when he chose to share our most private and intimate conversations with my family and one of my friends. The damage that this caused was almost irreversible. Although this caused me to sink deeper into an emotional and physical rock bottom, I made the decision not to share the information he told me about others. Though very tempting, I chose not to because I didn't think that people would believe me and I wanted to respect his friendships and relationships with others even though he didn't respect mine. This is a decision that I have somewhat regretted but would it have really changed anything? Retaliation wasn't the answer.

One afternoon as I gazed into my bathroom mirror, over-weight and depressed, I asked myself "How did I get here?" As I prayerfully and anxiously waited for the doctor's office to call me with lab results, I began to pray. When the phone rang, I could barely muster the strength to answer it. I was at the brink of devastation. As I reluctantly answered, the soft voice on the other side relayed that all was well. By this time, I had already ended this terrible relationship. But, it was at that point that I decided that I must live my life differently. This included my professional life as a nurse and also the relationships that I was involved in. I was tired of the emotional rollercoaster and thought it was beyond time for a change.

Victorious & Transparency

What does it mean to be *victorious*? Does it mean surviving a traumatic experience all to live and tell the story or does it mean being successful at conquering every huddle in life?

What does it mean to be *transparent*? Does it mean being able to see through something or does it mean being completely honest with oneself. Transparency makes us take the masks of "all is well" or "I am doing great" off. Transparency forces us to have an honest and very difficult conversation with ourselves, a conversation that perhaps reveals weakness, insufficiencies and doubts, but will help to bandage the wounds.

My Childhood

In order to fully understand where I am headed, you would have to understand the journey that got me here. I am from small town East Texas, population "I know everyone and we are all cousins." You may laugh, but this is seriously how it is. My hometown consists of about 6000+ people and probably five red lights uniformly placed down Hwy 80. Sports, particularly football, rule here. There are a lot of small mom and pop type businesses in town, mostly consisting of antiques. Unfortunately, there are not a lot of resources in town for medical professionals. So, it was imperative that I looked to the next larger cities for college and work. The one tiny hospital that we once had closed in the 90s forcing our nurses, including my mom, to look for work elsewhere.

The small historic neighborhood where I grew up sits geographically on the outskirts of town. It is made up of cousins and close friends. The running joke growing up was you better leave in order to find love because you will end up marrying your cousin. But this little community, which we fondly call Red Rock, created who I am at the core as a person. Hot summer days were spent going from door to door playing with the neighborhood children or riding my bike from sun up to sun down. Sundays were spent at church, sometimes all-day long. I can still hear the old COGIC church that sat behind our house. I can hear feet patting on old wooden floors. I can see the mothers with their wide brimmed hats, pearls, and gloves. I can hear the choir in tune with the tambourines and organ. Everyone knew everyone, so there was little fear that we, as children, would ever be hurt in anyway. The elders watched us and made sure we did what we were supposed to. It was the essence of a village mentality. My grandparents were well respected members of our community and so was my immediate little family. My brother and I lived the good life consisting of sports, academic activities, love and respect. Our family wasn't rich by any means, but we were what's considered "well off." My mom was a nurse who fought hard to rise up the clinical ladder. My dad was a hard-working man in the foundry industry. And both also had legal side sources of income as well. I quickly learned as a child that we had it a little better than a lot of children and we were regarded as having it all together. My childhood at home was mainly carefree, which perhaps laid a deadly foundation for the defeats that I would later face in life. At school was a different situation. I was considered a nerd, a tomboy and not cool. I stood out sometimes like a sore thumb. I often felt very uncomfortable around other females because I felt like I didn't add up at all. I wasn't the popular cheerleader with the cute body that all of the guys were after. I was the athletic nerd who made good grades and followed the rules. I know…...it makes for a boring story. On top of that, came a very poor self-esteem and body image that I still tussle with today. My teachers loved me because I made good grades and did as expected, but I never felt like I quite fit in with my peers. This was exacerbated during the 7th grade. A disagreement with a few girls in my class, exploded to a whole race of people turning on me. Luckily, these were the days before internet and mass shootings. I dealt with the bullying by running and sinking into darkness. Lunches and birthdays were often spent alone. This continued into high school. This experience has shaped a lot of who I am today. I still struggle with forming outgoing relationships with people sometimes. People laugh at me now when I explain that I actually am kind of shy and it takes some time for me to mentally and emotionally warm up. People see my now as being sociable and put together. And, I will admit, compared to where I once was, I am doing a lot better; however, I continue to be a work in progress. During these years, I developed a sense of humor to try to cope. I felt like if I could make people laugh, then they would like me.

Life & Nursing

I entered nursing school for my associate's degree the year after graduating from high school. I was focused and ready for a new beginning. I managed to complete all of my pre-requisite classes within a year and started nursing school the fall semester of 2003. I was very young. I was so young that I almost felt like an embryo, just floating through life waiting to be fertilized with experience. The majority of my classmates were much older, more skilled and more experienced. I, at this point, was just trying to figure out what I was going to eat from day to day.

During this time, my parents were divorcing. The aftermath was damaging. Our once spotless image imploded right before my eyes. I found comfort in my first real love. This gentleman was perfect. He fit pretty much all of the desires on my wants list. He was charming, smart, kind, funny and just perfect. We truly fit or at least that is what I thought. Unbeknownst to me, he was actually living a completely double life. Now I must admit, there were a lot of pieces to the puzzle that never fully added up. I can admit that I ignored a lot of warning signs, partially because that is what I thought I was supposed to do, plus I didn't want to get rid of what I thought was the perfect catch. I was in a real relationship now. Wasn't I supposed to be dedicated and compromising, just like I had been in my school work? Wasn't I supposed to help him become the best man he could be?

I also became sick during nursing school, which forced me to have to have surgery right before my last semester. A few months later, I landed my first nursing job in Tyler, about 30 minutes away from home. I was interested in several positions, but I had interviewed for just a few. I chose a telemetry position on a brand-new wing in the hospital. Everything was shiny and fresh, much different than the urine infested facilities for which I had trained. I felt good about the position because the managers were warm and welcoming. They explained that it was much better for me to get my training on their floor where the nurse-to-patient ratio was often 6:1, opposed to going into the intensive care unit because it would be easier to transition to a smaller patient ratio later. I naively accepted not completely understanding how this decision would affect my professional career.

A few weeks after graduation, I started my new position. I was barely 21. My life before nursing was so virginal, innocent and caring. I was probably as naïve as it gets. Smart, but naïve. I truly believed that most people were nice and wouldn't possibly want to hurt anyone else.

I spent the first few weeks with a preceptor. She was very smart and experienced. But she was also unprofessional and uncaring. At this time in my life, I couldn't deal with her attitude and I quickly started to drown professionally. I spoke to my manager about this and I was reassigned a new preceptor who was equally as smart, but caring and nurturing. After several months, she helped me to stay afloat in what would become a rollercoaster career.

By the end of my two-year contract in summer of 2007, I was personally and professionally burnt out to the point that I spontaneously quit that job and moved to the Dallas-Ft. Worth area. Immaturely, I packed all that I could in my Pontiac G6 and disappeared. After I secured a job and place to stay, I tried to settle into some form of a new routine while I anxiously awaited my first love to join me. The wait turned into two years of lies and deceit until I gained the strength to end the relationship. During this time, my job turned from Heaven to Hell. Now I know this may sound familiar and you might be thinking, "Haven't we already covered this story before?" My answer would be yes…. sort of. When I entered into early adulthood, my carefree pure childhood caught up with me. I quickly realized that I was trying to live perfectly in an imperfect world, which set up a recipe of not being able to deal with the imperfections of others. At my jobs, this manifested into misery and frustration. In my relationships, this manifested into depression, sorrow and timid behaviors. So yes, I would have to admit that I have kept falling into the same hamster wheel of bad jobs and bad relationships throughout the years.

So back to the story from 2012. Once I made up my mind to stop foolish behaviors and to live life more abundantly, emotional freedom and clarity started to manifest. It is a choice to live life happy with peace and contentment. This was something that I had to recognize.

Within the next few years, I started my crafting business which allowed my mind to open and creative freedom to flow. It was at this time that I realized that comfort was setting up a deadly concoction for professional stagnation. Crafting helped me to refocus from the stressors of work and more on my God-given talents. Also, I lost a ton of weight, cut my hair in order to go natural, spiritually refocused on my connection and relationship with God and started to travel and experience life outside of Texas. And yes, within this time, I ran across a few more bad situations, but I dismissed them quickly to avoid years of emotional turmoil. It was during this time that I discovered my calling in nursing for entrepreneurship, mentorship and health promotion. These things really stabilized my career on a track of professional growth and freedom. It gave me control and autonomy over my own career choices and decisions that would later benefit me.

Lessons

So thus far, I have learned: (1) to never trust another man ever again and (2) play the lotto so that I can quit working these jobs that give me zero satisfaction. I'm just kidding, but I can say there have been a lot of lessons to learn and still plenty more to go. Sometimes, I talk to God and ask, "Have I learned the lessons that You want me to learn?"

I can honestly and say that I have learned that:

.....I was tired of living prisoner to my thoughts of inadequacy.

.....being faithful and trusting of God's purpose in my life is valuable. It takes patience and commitment, but it is well worth the victory.

.....to let go and truly allow God to do His job.

.....being obedient to what God has called me to do will bless someone else, and I will get blessed in the process, too.

.....greatness takes focus, discipline, strength, endurance and perseverance.

.....to avoid mediocre mindset like the plague.

.....that a person can treat you no worse than you allow them to.

.....my life operates best for me when I am in balance mentally, spiritually, professionally and emotionally. I try to protect this balance at all costs.

.....if you don't see yourself as God sees you, you will allow anyone to mistreat you.

.....that being connected to God through relationship is the best thing I could have ever done.

Closing

In closing, we all will go through things in life for this is inevitable. It is how we react and what we make of it that is most important. Whether it is a job, a relationship, illness, or disappointments, we all will encounter something throughout our lifetime that will rock our boats of stability. Will we be strong enough to bounce back? Will we be capable of claiming victory? Will we be able to testify of the goodness of the Lord? And will we learn the lessons that are to be learned? These are questions we must ask ourselves.

Honestly, a lot of the situations that I have encountered are due to my own personal shortcomings. Issues of doubt, frustration, and nervouse behaviors all have played their roles. Oftentimes, I must take a step back to regroup and ask God for His patience and guidance. As I write and allow the tears to roll down my cheeks and permeate the white pages of this book, I am reminded of what purpose is about. My story is one of sorrow, but it is also one of victory, triumph and success. It is the choice to live happily and freely in the midst of God's purpose that gives me peace.

Currently, I just endured a small storm. I know, I know…you are thinking, "Another issue?" Will she ever get it together?" My pastor always says that either you are about to be in a storm, currently in one, or just coming out from one. Through transparency, I can admit that a lot of my relationships professionally have crumbled due to lack of handling stress and frustration appropriately. I expected this storm because I am in nursing school for the third time. The devil has a slick way of trying to attack you when you are doing something good. When I mentor students and new nurses, I remind them that they will likely be attacked during this season; therefore, they must be prepared with the armor of God.

I am truly a victorious nurse and woman of God because I decided to follow the King, step out on faith and make life work for me. One of the best things I could have done (and am still doing) is to have learned to forgive myself and to see me as God does. Being victorious is not a static phrase, but one that is constantly evolving and maturing. This means that if you continue to allow God to use you and continue to be connected to Him, you will taste and see how sweet His victories are over and over again. I named this book **TRANSPARENCY** in order to be real and authentic to myself, for in order to claim victory, one must be open and honest from within. This means giving permission to be wrong, to be hurt and to be healed. Life is a precious process and trusting the process is imperative.

Victory is mine. To God be the GLORY!

Biography

Alvionna Brewster has been a registered nurse since 2005, primarily specializing in cardiovascular care and preventative medicine. In 2015, Alvionna started Black Nurse Entrepreneurs in order to network, empower, and encourage entrepreneurship amongst black nurses. Currently, Alvionna is pursuing a Master's Degree in Nursing Education with hopes of opening a nursing education center with a focus on community and clinical educational resources. She is passionate about the success of new nurses, helping patients successfully understand and manage disease processes and the advancement of African-Americans. In her free time, you will catch her creating crafts for her first business, The Creative Brewtique.

To contact the author:

FB: https://www.facebook.com/alvionna.brewster

IG: https://www.instagram.com/alvionna/

LinkedIn: https://www.linkedin.com/in/alvionna-brewster-bsn-rn-24067953/

Acknowledgments

I dedicate this book to my first loves, my parents Mr. Luster Robert Ingram and Mrs. Dorothy Yarbrough Ingram-Traylor, who have loved me unconditionally. To my grandmothers Hattie McNeil Yarbrough and Bertha McAfee Ingram who were the strongest and yet most humble women that I have ever known. To my loving strong husband Mr. George L. Borens, who from day one, has seen me for who I truly am, and it has always been enough. To my three sons Anthony, Shed, and Brandon; they make me go harder and stronger every day to be the mother and friend that they deserve. Finally to my many mentors who's paths I've crossed over the years, you have helped me to grow and become the proud nurse and person that I am today.

Paula

My Victorious Transformation

By Paula Ingram-Borens, AD, LVN

Tears of anguish, disparity and so many shattered dreams. I look out of the window of the family car, not knowing where my tears ended and the rain began.

I don't know exactly where to start the story, but this was the worst of many losses that I had to face in my young adult years. Why did it feel that I was not only burying my daughter, but burying my soul and my heart along with my future?

The ache and sadness that I still can feel, knowing that I have kept a secret for over thirty-three years. I keep it hidden, thinking that one day it will just dissolve and, maybe, simply disappear. Needless to say, it has never disappeared, just like a cancerous, gangrenous sore, it made everything in my life sick. So I will begin my story ….

Ceremony after ceremony, my senior year of high school was a culmination of pomp and circumstance. One event after the other: senior pictures, senior trips, senior coronation, senior prom and, to top it off, I was chosen to be a debutante. I absolutely loved school; education was a top priority in our home. I gravitated naturally to reading and adored books and the journey on which they took me. I would finish a three hundred page book in one day. Great authors are able to lace their stories with suspense and desire and I wanted, always, to know more about the characters.

Love was even in the air! At sweet seventeen, to be in love with your best friend and to have the love and admiration of your family, parents and teachers…how exhilarating to have everything right in the world in placed in your hands!

Except this night, everything changed. The night my assailant pulled my formal dress over my head and held me captive in the fullness of it. I wasn't able to see, move, or fight off my attacker. What did I do to bring this on? All I could do is beg God to help me. I maybe could have understood it if it had been a stranger. But, this was not a stranger. In fact, handpicked by my parents, he was a supposed gentleman with high class and morals.

My silence scared me - who could I tell? No one would believe me over him. So, I kept quiet and internalized it all. My parents were successful in their careers and it was my job to keep me together. The remainder of my senior year was a blur. I felt myself slipping more and more into a deep dark space that wouldn't allow me to come up for air. It wouldn't allow me to share with anyone what had occurred.

Over the next six months, I pulled away from everyone who was close to me. I even stopped going to church, which was not me at all. I loved worship; however, at this time, I felt like I needed to hide. I not only hid from God, but I hid from my parents, my friends, and eventually, even the one I adored. No one knew what to do with me and eventually I gave up on myself. I told myself many things: "You're not worthy of love," "No one really wanted you in the first place," "You know that you were too fat, too tall, too opinionated, too complex and, definitely now, too damaged."

With this type of mindset and no self-esteem, I started college. Everyone was oblivious to my silence. I was not emotionally or mentally prepared for school. Everyday was the same endless battle. I was trying to fit in, not really knowing whom to trust. Longing and wanting to have the security of my old life again. Not able to focus on any lectures, classes, homework, band practices. I lost over forty pounds in less than a two month period. I didn't enjoy life or anyone. I was just going through the motions of getting dressed, showing up and wandering through my day. It breaks my heart all over again, to even have these memories resurface. Everyone talked about how good I looked now. The only person that paid attention to me, knowing that my extreme weight loss was not healthy, was my grandmother.

My lifelines were two people who accepted me broken and thought my servitude was just me being quirky. Every once in awhile, these two could make the old me resurface. But they accepted me just as I was - a shell of a person. They are now reading this for the first time, as you are. I am still so grateful to these two. Even though I could never open up to tell them about my past, I know that they both loved me through it all. Throughout everything and through the years, they are still dear to my heart.

It is so true that when you start spiraling down, it never ends. The bottom will continue to drop, especially if you don't take the time to deal with your issues. You also will subconsciously draw into your life the worst people. It's almost like they are headhunters looking for their next prey. However, when you are in a vulnerable state, the last thing you need in your life is someone worse off than you are. At this time, I was so lonely that I would accept any form of affection. What was so sad is that I thought they were genuine.

One particular person would actually run to the band hall every day to help me with my instrument and carry my books. I wouldn't give him the time of day at this point. But eventually, over summer break, he wore me down by calling me everyday and saying the right words. I couldn't wait until the fall semester began, so that I could see him face to face. Eventually, we were the campus couple, and I was off limits to everyone else.

He was miraculously everything that I had desired, or so I thought. I am only sharing this with you because the devil comes in many disguises - especially ones that you desire to have. A few months later, I was pregnant and he asked me to marry him. I said yes. I just wanted to be accepted and loved; I was so naive that I never thought about the fact that we were both college students with no jobs, no plans and definitely no future for us or a child.

Needless to say, it didn't take long for the gossip to start. My girlfriends were the first to notify me that my beau was escorting a pregnant girl around campus before the homecoming football game. When I asked him about it, he said that was his sister. When I reported this back to my friends, they looked at me, crazy, and said, "Is his sister white?"

The truth sometimes will slap you dead in the face. It turned out that he had a fiance in his hometown. She was pregnant with their second child. Their oldest was already two years old. My reality was shattered; how did I let this happen? I had been to his parents home several times. His mom adored me. She even tailored outfits for us to wear to church. No one…I mean no one…told me anything about this other woman and definitely not about the children.

Struggling with this crazy situation, I was not able to talk again to my parents. How could I explain this fiasco to anyone, especially them? Ashamed, I didn't want to have this baby. I had even contemplated having an abortion. My grandmother, however, wasn't having any part of that discussion. She said, "God doesn't make any mistakes. You have to trust and hold on that it's going to work itself out and, if you do something to this baby, He may never bless you again." I understood what she was saying and I trusted her. My mother was grateful for my change and promised that my family would help me. I was still ashamed and my education faltered even worse. I didn't want to talk to anyone - especially my real friends. No matter what they stuck by me.

Eventually, I accepted that I was going to have this baby and just keep on going to school. I was 21 weeks when my water broke. My mom and dad were both at work. I didn't know what the significance was until I called my mother and she said, "It's too early! Are you sure your water broke?" Once I made it to the hospital, I was taken immediately upstairs and admitted. They placed me on bed rest. My doctor told me that I needed to be in the hospital as long as I could, so that my baby could get stronger and survive on her own. Every day, they would do sonograms and say she was fine. One morning, I woke up and I didn't feel her moving and I started crying. They checked her fetal heart tones and there wasn't one. They prepared me for surgery.

I was allowed to hold her. She was so perfect and already had a head full of hair. Why did this happen to her? She deserved so much more. My only daughter, with whom I would never get to bond, for whom I would never be able to buy dresses and shoes, or just be her number one cheerleader in life. But the funeral was worse, seeing the pain that I caused myself and my parents with my decisions. I promised that I would never let them down again.

It took me a year to get myself back up and form a game plan that would allow me to move on. My best friend in high school decided that we would move to Arlington and attend UTA. I went along with this plan, mainly to get out of Hallsville. I found a job working as a CNA. Working at Arlington Memorial Hospital, I was exposed to different cultures and ethnicity. I was one of only three American born people who worked on my floor. Along with learning about my coworkers, I was also exposed to a work ethic that I admired and, to this day, I attribute these people for my diligence in completing anything that I start and try to do it well.

My charge nurse was a military nurse. She had so many awesome abilities - as a human being, as a nurse and as a military person. I had never been around anyone like her before. She had even written some books; that was not something that I thought nurses did, so I was totally fascinated. The more I was around her and the other nurses on my floor, the more I knew in my heart that I wanted to be just like them. I wanted to become a nurse. I wanted to be smart and someone of substance.

At this time, I was living in a world of my circumstances and nothing that had occurred up until this point was my decision. I felt like if I could come up with a game plan, and start being proactive instead of reactive, that my life would change for the better. However, at this time, I really didn't know how to make things change for me. No one outside of my immediate family had ever helped me, nor mentored me to make better choices. Both of my grandmothers had instilled into me a strong spiritual background. I knew that I hadn't praised or worshiped in a long time, but I talked to the only being I knew that would hear me - my God. I promised him if he would help me out one more time, then I would start going nonstop. I know that you are not supposed to barter with God, but this was different; this was my vow. I was praising Him for things I have never seen nor could ever imagined to happen in my life. For some reason, I knew it would come to pass. I knew, at that moment, God had never intended for me to be where I was. If I just followed his calling and allowed him to open the doors, everything would be alright.

My oldest son was two years old and I was not happy with his father or my circumstances. I knew, deep down, that he wasn't happy with me, either. We only had one car and he was the owner and reiterated that our money was mostly his money. I knew that if I didn't make a first step that I would be miserable for the rest of my life. So I called my father and said, "Daddy, can I come home?" I heard him sobbing and his next sentence was, "I've been waiting for you to call." I packed all night long, making sure that I had all of my baby's belongings. The next day, my brother drove up, sent by my dad. We loaded what we could of our belongings and left the rest. When I say "left the rest," there was my bedroom set, my living room set, washer and dryer and 99% of my clothes and shoes. I didn't care. I knew it was time to go.

The very next day, I applied for a job at a local nursing home and hired on the spot. After leaving there, I went directly to the Kilgore Vocational Nursing School in Longview and applied for the upcoming program. I took the entrance exam a few weeks later.

The waiting period was the worst. Some of my coworkers told me that they had been on the waiting list for 2-3 years. The school only accepted 25 students per semester and of those, only 2-3 were minorities. I just kept on working, even though I hated my surroundings and the mentality of the staff who worked at this nursing home was deplorable.

In the back of my mind, I just kept praying and saying, "When I finish nursing school, I will be an example for my nursing assistants to follow. I will never ask someone to do something that I wouldn't do myself."

The first miracle started with me being accepted into the very next program start up. I received points for working at the nursing home and having experience at the hospital in Arlington. I was also told that I scored the highest on the entrance exam. This really shocked me, since my prior failures in college had not prepared me for success and, at this time, I had been out of high school for 7 years.

The second miracle happened to be an opening that came up for me at Good Shepherd Home Health. The requirements were that I would have only one patient for whom I would care 4 hours - from 3 pm - 7 pm every day, Monday through Friday. My patient was the sweetest person ever, and her house was 2 minutes away from the college. My schedule worked out perfectly because my classes ended at 3 pm every day. My new job also allowed me to be a sitter, for 12 hour shifts, on Saturdays and Sundays. I had full time hours with full time benefits for me and my son.

The third miracle was my new job provided free daycare at a prestigious school next to Trinity Episcopal School. It was just across the street from Good Shepherd Hospital and only a few blocks from my nursing school. It was funny how my sisters, brother and my son would load up in my Dad's Bronco and head out. We would drop my son off at daycare, then they would drop me off at Kilgore Longview Center and the three of them would head to Kilgore Jr. College in Kilgore, Texas.

I eventually bought the ugliest car ever, but she was mine; paid in full. She got me through until graduation the following year. The week of graduation, I bought myself a white Honda Accord. I thought I was balling. Graduation was incredible, the ceremony was held on a Friday. I immediately was transferred by my hospital from home health to the Med-surgical floor, known then as A-300.

I started work the very next Monday.

I learned so much the first year as a nurse. The experiences that you learn on a medical floor are priceless. We use to say, if you can work A-300, you can work anywhere. So far, this has been true. After working there a year, I was allowed to transfer to the Emergency Department. I absolutely thrived and worked there for 9 more years. I also met my husband. We were automatic soulmates…but that is another story.

It has been over 25 years since I graduated from nursing school. I made up my mind, with the help of God, to pursue and accomplish other goals. Even though I got married and was not able to work full time when all three of my children were young, I did return to school after the two oldest were in college. I graduated from Tyler Jr. College, Phi Theta Honor Society and Cum Laude with my Associates Degree in 2015. At this time, I have one more year to graduate with my Bachelor's Degree in Healthcare Management from Walden University. I was inducted into Walden's Upsilon Phi Delta Honor Society in December of 2017. I give God all of the praise for awakening in me the desire to be a role model for my family and for young ladies who may have been distracted and derailed by life's circumstances.

In conclusion, if this story helps anyone that desires to move or transform their own lives, I just want you to know that God can help transform you, too. After all, he was able to transform someone like me, who had lost her heart, spirit and all hope behind rape, death and conditions of hopelessness. I don't want my story to be in vain. Nor do I want to embarrass myself or my family in telling it. I hope that by sharing my story and my testimony, I will be able to help anyone to not give up on his/her dreams. All my help comes from the Lord and I do give Him all the glory and all the praise for this victorious transformation.

Biography

Paula Ingram-Borens, has been a nurse for over 25 years. She has over nine years experience in the Emergency Department. She has worked in Occupational Medicine for 15 years, where she was chosen as Exemplary Nurse of the Year in 2007. Soon after, she was promoted from staff nurse to Employer Relations Coordinator for her employer, where she developed the Health and Wellness/ Random Drug Program. At this time she is the contracted nurse for one of the major employers in Longview, Texas. Paula is also the proud President/CEO/Founder of the Longview Texas Chapter of Black Nurses Rock. She is married to her soulmate and biggest cheerleader, George Borens and the proud mother of three sons Anthony, Shed, and Brandon.

Nursepborens@gmail.com for speaking or event request.

Acknowledgements

We would like to thank God first and foremost for giving us this opportunity to share our testimony and allowing us to give hope to others despite life's circumstances. We thank our husbands, John Hill and EJ Jordan, for their love and support while writing this book. To Emare and Elija Jordan, thank you for your love and support and pushing me to be better a mother and woman.

We would like to thank our parents for instilling in us the determination to achieve anything we put our mind to and always being supportive in all of our endeavors. To our sister Shundra Mack, thank you for your assurance in our ability to accomplish this dream. To our nephews, Shaquil and Michael Jr Mack and niece, Shaniqua Mack, thank you for constantly being there while we went through cancer and never complained about anything that was asked of you.

Shanetra and Shaletra

Leap of Faith

By Dr. Shanetra Hodge-Hill and Dr. Shaletra Jordan

Have you ever wondered what is God's purpose for your life, especially when deciding on a future career? We decided to follow in the footsteps of our older sister by becoming Registered Nurses (RNs). As RNs, we have a compassion for helping people reach a state of well-being, whether it is physically, emotionally, spiritually, or psychologically. While going through clinical in our nursing program, we decided that we wanted to become critical care trauma RNs. In 2004, we decided to accept a job at Grady Memorial Hospital in Atlanta, Georgia. This was a well-known level one trauma unit that would prepare us for our future endeavors in the nursing field. We enjoyed the challenges and complexities of being critical care trauma RNs.

There's no words that can describe saving and making a difference in someone else's life during one of their most critical moments. In those moments, we knew that God had placed us in the nursing field for a greater purpose. By seeing and taking of care of critical patients, we were building a closer relationship with God. We recall many times praying for patients to make it through the critical state and eventually leave the hospital to go back to their homes and families. As a critical care trauma RN, you are the patient's and family's support system during those difficult times. We believe that during those difficult moments, where critical decisions need to be made for the patient's well-being, the family needs to be reassured that the healthcare team is doing everything to help their family member.

While working at Grady, we gained great experience, but we knew that God had something greater in store for us, which led us to become travel RNs. Travel nursing allowed us to see different aspects of healthcare, as well as new technological advances. As we travelled to many hospitals across the country, we decided that we wanted to take our nursing career to the next level. We began researching various advanced nursing opportunities. Shaletra remembered the clinical educator at Grady stating that one day we would become Certified Registered Nurse Anesthetists (CRNAs). We began researching various CRNA schools, as well as shadowing CRNAs at the facility in which we were currently working. We both prepared for the requirements for admission into the CRNA program, which included taking the Graduate Record Examination (GRE) and obtaining Critical Care Registered Nurse (CCRN) certification. As we were waiting for an interview from the CRNA program, devastation happened in our lives.

August 2009, our lives' changed, but our faith would be tested and become stronger. Shanetra was playing with Shaletra's two year old son, when a sharp, numbing pain went down the right side of her body. I was able to reach over and grab my phone to call my sister for help. When you are an RN, you tend to self-diagnose yourself; therefore, many thoughts went through my mind while waiting for my sister to arrive home from work. As she rushed me to the emergency room, I just began to pray that everything would be fine. As I was in the computed tomography (CT) scan, I continued to pray and think positive thoughts. When the physician walked into the room, she stated that I had a stomach mass and that I would be immediately going to St. Luke's Hospital to be admitted.

At that moment, I was overwhelmed and consumed with many emotions because I didn't understand why this was happening. As an RN, you spend a lot of time taking care of other people that sometimes you forget to take care of yourself. During the next several weeks, I had multiple biopsies of the stomach mass and the results were negative. I continued to focus on advancing my career, despite the current circumstances that I was in. My family continued to be my strength during this time. After the exploratory laparotomy, I was notified that I had stage 4 aggressive Hodgkin's Lymphoma.

After that, I started chemotherapy immediately. I had to get prepared mentally, psychologically, and spiritually for the road ahead of me, but my mom and sisters would be there to support me through this difficult time. We decided to postpone attending CRNA school until after the chemotherapy treatment. As months went by, we continued to prepare for attending CRNA school, so we decided to reapply to several schools. In March of 2010, I completed my chemotherapy treatment, which was a moment I had been looking forward to since being diagnosed. While I was getting my clearance of being cancer free at MD Anderson, Shaletra was next door at St. Luke's undergoing surgery to see if she has cancer as well.

In December 2009, we were driving when Shaletra felt a lump underneath her clavicle bone. She underwent a CT scan and her doctor noticed enlarged lymph nodes, but nothing to be concerned about at the time until one day she was driving and could not grip the steering wheel. After another CT scan was done, it was found that Shaletra had a mass near her heart and a supraclavicular mass.

A supraclavicular lymph node biopsy was done, but due to the unrelenting pain, the procedure was aborted and a biopsy under general anesthesia was done. We did not understand why this was happening again, but God had a purpose for this. The results came back and it was Stage II Hodgkin's Lymphoma. Although nobody wants cancer, we had to thank God that we were blessed with a cancer that could be easily treated with chemotherapy and, if it came back, the treatment would be a stem cell transplant. Before starting chemotherapy, we took a trip to Mexico just to ease our minds and enjoy life before tackling cancer.

In May 2010, Shaletra started chemotherapy. After seeing what my sister went through, I was somewhat prepared for what I would endure. I did not have time for self pity because I had a 2 year old son who needed me. I continued to work full time and be the best mom that I could possibly be. I endured chemotherapy ever other week and, during this time, I found my strength and God gave me peace. At the time, I was working in interventional radiology, so I encountered many patients coming in to have their port-a-catheters placed for chemotherapy treatment. During these moments, God allowed me to be a testimony to my patients. I learned that until you go through something, then you can't fully understand what it feels like. I saw my sister go through chemotherapy, but I did not fully understand it until I went through it myself. I had moments during my treatment where I was asking God, "Why me?" Chemotherapy takes a toll on your body because you can smell it coming through your skin and out of your body, it changes your taste buds and appetite, and it makes you feel tired and weak. I would get chemotherapy every other Friday, and a neupogen shot every other Saturday, for 6 months. After the neupogen shot, my body would feel cold and jittery, but I was still super mom at home and super nurse at work. I took organic nutrients to help build up my immune system and give me energy to continue on. I stopped focusing on the cancer and started focusing on my Healer. I became more prayful as well as having a more positive outlook about my treatment plan. I had a mass near my heart, and the oncologist wanted to do radiation on top of chemotherapy. I told the doctor to let me pray about it and that I would let him know my decision, because radiation would be a weekly treatment and increase my chance of other comorbidities due to the location of the mass. I prayed and I prayed and then God showed up because now my scans revealed that the mass near my heart was completely gone, so therefore no radiation was needed. Thank you Jesus! However, I still had to finish the chemotherapy. My faith in God got me through that, as well as my sister, through this trying time in our lives. My oncologist declared me to be cancer free in November 2010 and just when we thought we had seen light at the end of the tunnel, darkness came about.

In April 2011, Shanetra's cancer returned. Here it is again like a dagger to our family's heart because instead of chemotherapy, I needed a stem cell transplant. Shaletra would have been a good match for me, but because she had cancer too, she could not be a donor. I had started the treatment process, which required me to go into the hospital every other week. During the transplant process, my body became so cold that the nurses had to wrap several blankets around me to keep me warm. My body became extremely weak, which led to me not eating or drinking from several days to weeks. I couldn't understand why God was allowing me to endure this. I cried so many nights, and I questioned God about this process. I knew him as a Healer because He healed me before from cancer, as well as my sister, so this was definitely a test of my faith. I had two choices, which included giving up or trusting God. I decided to trust God and declare healing over myself. I prayed more than I cried. I stopped playing victim and started to walk into my survivorship. I found strength that I never knew that I had, and it was all due to my faith in God because I understood that He wouldn't put more on me than I could bare. I had learned to trust the process. Shaletra and I decided to continue to pursue advanced degrees in nursing. While I was finishing up my treatment process, we started interviewing at various CRNA schools throughout the country. Our faith in God during the process of cancer treatment resulted in a door opening for us to further our career and not to give up on our hopes and dreams in life.

In January 2012, we started CRNA School at Arkansas State University. It was a true blessing for the both of us to be accepted and have the opportunity to go to school together. Shanetra was still recovering from her treatment so she would periodically have to go back to Houston for check-ups. We studied and prayed together. Our first clinical rotation was in a rural area in Arkansas where there weren't many minorities, but when God has a plan for your life, he places his hedge of protection around you and guides you through every situation in your life. Normally, the clinical rotation is only for 3 months, but the chief of medical services called the Director of our program and asked if she would allow us to do another 3 months there. She was amazed that he asked for that request, as well as proud. That clinical rotation prepared us for the next rotation because the majority of the people that came from that rotation lacked knowledge and fell behind the rest of the students, but we left ahead of everyone else. God places you in the right places at the right time. We graduated from Arkansas State University with a GPA of 3.9 and a Masters degree. In 2016, we started and graduated with our DNP from Chatham University.

We trusted God through every process in our lives. Yes, our faith wavered at times as we didn't understand why we had to endure this situation because no one in our family had this type of cancer, but we decided to take a leap of faith and trust the process. Our leap of faith resulted in us obtaining CRNA degrees as well our DNP. Cancer is a game changer for many people's lives, but you must continue to trust in the ultimate Healer, God. Faith is what will help keep your head above water and to get you through every situation in your life. Allow this testimony to be a testimony of how we overcame and took a leap of faith into what God had destined for our lives.

Biography

Shaletra Jordan and Shanetra Hodge-Hill are doctorally prepared CRNAs whom now live and work in the greater Houston area. They were Critical Care Trauma RNs for 8 years and CRNAs for 3 plus years. They obtained their Master's in Nurse Anesthesia from Arkansas State University in Jonesboro, Arkansas and Doctorate of Nursing Practice from Chatham University in Pittsburgh, Pennsylvania. During the advancement of their nursing career, they have had several cancer treatments for Hodgkin's lymphoma. As cancer survivors, they are able to help their surgical patients maintain a positive outlook while going through their own cancer treatments. They have also inspired others to never give up on their career goals and dreams despite the challenges in life. During their free time, Shaletra likes spending time with her husband and two boys, while Shanetra likes spending time with her husband and travelling the world.

Acknowledgements

I offer expressions of gratitude to those who encouraged me to start my journey into the healthcare field; and once well on my way, to all family and friends who continued to offer reassurance, prayer, words of advice, and positivity toward my nursing career. To my amazingly supportive husband, Derrick, I appreciate you more than words can express, as your unwavering leadership, faith and wisdom has carried me many times when life's obstacles were ever so present! Last, but certainly not least, to The Most High God, I thank you for simply allowing me to be a part of this journey called life and confirming your guiding presence every step of the way!

Santisha

Stethoscope and A DREAM

By Santisha L. Walker, MSN, RN, CWC

Life Is But a Dream

Dreams. We all have them. From childhood until our last day on this earth, we all aspire to something. When most people hear the word "dream" they think of images or feelings experienced while asleep; but a dream could also include something one may desire to do, or hope to become. Dreams often allow us to detach from our reality and envision an end goal, with the hopes of achieving what's dear to our heart. It's human nature to dream. It keeps us moving forward. Life is an ongoing journey, blossoming in every moment, lending to us the opportunity to explore, feel, touch, taste and dream!

Hindsight Is 20/20

I've always been a dreamer. I remember, as a young girl, visualizing my future, knowing I would intricately "help" others. But who knew that my dream of helping others would lead to nursing? Becoming a nurse never came to mind. It was not until I had an "ah-ha" moment during college that nursing came into my view. While engaging in an on-campus conversation, at UNC-Greensboro, with two girls who I would socialize with through a mutual friend and who were already a part of the nursing program, something ignited inside of me that shifted my desire towards nursing. I was in my junior year of college and I had already been accepted into the Joseph M. Bryan School of Business and Economics program. Instead of delaying graduation by three years to pursue nursing, I decided to proceed with my business degree. I never shared with anyone what I experienced during the on-campus conversation; however, a few years later, I wish I had sought mentorship, as I ended up pursing nursing nonetheless. After working in the insurance industry for four years, I decided it was time to fuel that initial on-campus spark and proceed with nursing.

I would advise anyone with a strong intuition towards a possible life changing situation, whether it involves a person, a career move, a relocation decision, etc., to not neglect your instinct toward that circumstance. There's a reason you are having those feelings. Seek counsel from a mentor, trusted friend, or family member. Be sure it is someone who knows you the best. They should not have an ulterior motive; and have nothing to gain or lose from your decision. This individual will help you think logically and provide a broad, life-long perspective regarding your decision.

Hurdles: Overcome and Keep Dreaming

Four years passed, and I completed nursing school. My pinning ceremony had finally arrived! "I can't believe I'm graduating from nursing school!" I said this aloud, with an enormous smile on my face and tears of joy in my eyes, as I donned myself head to toe in the required all white attire. Getting to this point was no easy task, and one of the most difficult experiences of my life. I had taken my pre-requisite classes at night, while working full-time, studying to pass placement tests for admission, and completing each class, lab and clinical, one assignment at a time. Anyone who has journeyed through nursing school understands the rigorous schedule, and the discipline and time commitment needed to succeed. Even with my husband's remarkable support and his ability to be self-sufficient, I had to remain focused enough to achieve my dream of completing nursing school.

When you are longing to achieve a dream, it is essential to make room in your life to prepare for that dream and do what is necessary to make that dream a reality. I had already allowed the opportunity to pass once before, and I made up my mind I would not let it pass again. I chose to progress onward, knowing if I put in the work and believed, I would be living my dreams.

After my pinning ceremony, I was confronted with the challenge of every nursing school graduate, passing the National Council Licensure Examination (NCLEX) and landing a job! I had not yet been offered a nursing position, like most of my classmates, and I was starting to worry. I told myself I had not come this far to not be able to overcome these last two hurdles. During this time of uncertainty, I began relying heavily on my spirituality, with much prayer and meditation on scripture. I also recalled my childhood dream of helping others, as well as the initial spark I felt during that conversation in college. All of these recollections were my foundation and fuel to remain positive and advance forward.

About one-month post-pinning ceremony, I interviewed with two hospital units and received an offer on a cardiovascular intermediate care step-down unit. I proudly accepted the position! I now had one last hurdle, passing the NCLEX. During this time, I discovered the power of vision boards, so I persistently kept optimistic images of my dream in my forefront. I continued to pray and became more disciplined in studying for the examination.

A week after taking the NCLEX, I received confirmation that I was officially a Registered Nurse! I did it! My dream had finally become my reality! This feeling was so surreal! I remember jumping up from the couch in my living room that evening, smiling and screaming as soon as I received the email. My husband was just as thrilled and smiled from ear to ear as he observed my excitement!

In that moment, I remembered all that it took to get to this point. I thanked God and then my husband for his priceless emotional, spiritual and financial support over the past four years.

It's one thing to experience an achievement because it is something you have been told you need to do to be successful, or secure a job, or run a family business, etc.; but it is a whole other feeling to acquire a victory because you know it is your calling. It is a dream, a vision you have had before you for quite some time. I did not choose nursing, but nursing chose me. I was ready to continue to fuel that initial spark from college. I was eager to begin the next phase in my life journey and get about the business of helping others!

Welcome to My Dream of Nursing: The Shock Factor

There I was. Walking through the hospital doors as a Registered Nurse (RN). I realized I now had a new level of responsibilities at all times, and that my life had changed completely. Nurses are leaders. We are one of the most trusted professionals. People take our words and actions seriously. We are the liaison between the healthcare profession and patients, our communities and families. I took my role as a nurse solemnly. I knew I had work to do and was looking forward to being a part of the care team in the nursing capacity. My first few days as an RN consisted of becoming acclimated to the unit, training and reviewing policies and procedures. While rounding, I also met many of the unit's staff. Being in good standing with other staff on the unit is vital to a successful start as a novice nurse.

After a few weeks of precepting, it was time for me to fly solo and manage my own shift. I'm a very organized person, so the task management aspect of nursing was of no concern to me. I had discovered my rhythm of receiving reports, completing vital signs and thorough assessments, documentation, administering medications, delegating to my nurse aids as needed, completing orders, etc. As weeks passed, my patient assignments became more complex, and I appreciated learning new interventions and nursing skills. I also adored the time I spent educating my patients about their health. I was undoubtedly in my element, and living my dream of intricately helping others and impacting their lives for the better.

I worked twelve-hour day shifts, which is tremendously busy in an acute care setting. Working on an intermediate step-down unit is even more fast paced, because of the patients' level of acuity. As time passed, there was an increase in my frustration during shifts. With the unit's busyness, as well as hospital wide changes to policies and procedures to achieve magnet status, increased required documentation, and simply being a novice nurse, I found myself not spending as much time with patients as I anticipated. During a large portion my shifts, I was glued to a computer screen. I was not lending as much therapeutic communication and patient education, from a total wellness perspective, as I would have liked. Although, as a nurse, I was still providing safe and competent care while completing the process of assessing, diagnosing, planning, implementing and evaluating, I felt my shift was spent chasing tasks, orders and a check-list.

Not only was I adjusting to changes in patient interaction, but I was also dealing with social characteristics of the unit. While most nurses were pleasant to interact with, there appeared to be a deviation in communication with many of the unit's veteran nurses. I am uncertain why these changes occurred, but I could only focus on my purpose of coming into work; and overlooking gossip, confusion, and cliques. Many times, I would retreat to the unit's respite room for down time, which worked very well for my mental wellness. I also would eat lunch alone at times to escape social complexities of the break room. In addition, I sought guidance from one of the staff members who served as a mentor for new graduate nurses.

After each shift, I was physically and mentally exhausted. The fast and furious energy of the day shift can take a toll on the body and mind; however, I was also fatigued from not feeling as if I "did enough" for my patients from a total wellness perspective. It's amazing how you can know you are purposed to do something, yet still experience a feeling of defeat while operating in your calling. You wouldn't think I would feel so burdened in the beginning of my nursing career, right?

Is This Normal?

Why am I feeling this way? Is it normal to feel "burnt out" this early into my nursing career, let alone any career? I've only been working as an RN for eight months. What is going on? I've worked entirely too hard to get to this point to lose interest this soon. Is this normal?

All of these questions were going through my mind before, during and after each shift, as well as on my days off. I was consumed with doubt to the point where I would cringe before my next shift. I was no longer connecting with my patients. I was losing my "why". I became the hustle and bustle of the unit; and felt robotic as I passed medication and checked off tasks. I indeed continued to provide safe, quality and competent care, but at what point was I integrating a true connection and promoting total wellness?

As I shared my concerns with my husband, he began encouraging me to rediscover my joy in nursing. He proposed that I search for another position in the nursing field. He made it sound so simple.

When he recommended this, I looked at him like he had two heads. He didn't understand the flow of a novice nurse's career. I had to remain in my hospital position for at least one year before I would even be considered for another position; at least this is what I had always been told by others. He did not comprehend this concept and encouraged me to apply for other positions anyway. I tell you, my husband had enough faith for the both of us to help carry me through my doubt and encourage me to keep dreaming!

I seized his advice and began applying for non-hospital positions. This process was a bit intimidating and discouraging, because most job descriptions asked for 3-5 years of experience. At one point, I felt trapped. I just knew I would be in my current position another two years, which would drain the life out of me. But none the less, I kept applying.

Over a course of two months, I received two interviews with an offer for both. I accepted the position providing a slower paced atmosphere and the chance to build a therapeutic relationship with patients. The position also offered a closer commute, stable hours and increased compensation. This new opportunity was immensely satisfying! If I would have listened to the status quo for new graduate nurses, I would have foregone continuing my nursing career in this new capacity. Once again, I chose to continue to dream!

Another Crossroad: Am I Still Dreaming?

After a year of settling into the neurology practice in the outpatient setting, I felt it was now time to pursue a more advanced degree. I had previously obtained my Associates Degree in Nursing (ADN) from Wake Technical Community College; and realized an ADN could potentially restrict my ability to advance in nursing, especially since many organizations nationwide are only hiring Bachelor of Science in Nursing (BSN) degree graduates (or higher). I envisioned myself eventually moving into the administrative role of nursing, and since I already held a BS in Business Administration, I decided to pursue a Master of Science in Nursing (MSN) Administration degree. As I began researching MSN programs, fear crept in. Questions flooded my mind. I asked, "What am I thinking? Who am I to think I can go from an ADN to an MSN? I don't even have a BSN! Most of my classmates are getting their BSN now and stopping there. Some are obtaining their BSN before their MSN. Why am I going for an MSN?" Yes, I was once again questioning myself while simultaneously choosing to dream. But, even with doubt present, as a dreamer, I cannot settle! If I have dreamt it, I have to work towards it until it has come into fruition. I eventually found a program that offered an RN to MSN degree at Gardner-Webb University. After preparation and placement tests, I was accepted into the program!

I continued to work full-time, and was comfortable with my stable schedule, steady paycheck and familiarity with staff, patients, policies, etc. I was as content as I could be. Well, that is until my husband came home one day and presented me with an opportunity which, little did I know, would wet my palate for something different. I found myself at another crossroad!

My husband was working as a design engineer at the headquarters of a large corporation, and one day he came home with pure excitement in his eyes! He mentioned the idea of him branching out into consulting. I loved the idea! We previously flirted with offering a platform for experts and professionals in our circle to provide their line of work to the community. We used to host annual Christmas parties throughout the city and Think Tanks at our home, and one day, noticed our guest list consisted of either current or aspiring business owners. And also professionals working in their field of expertise. Thus, the notion of being a consultant and providing resources for others was not new.

We further discussed his thoughts and created a practical business model. My husband then asked if I had ever considered being a nurse consultant. I immediately said "no". I informed him I was not interested, but would help him operate the company. He accepted my "no" in that moment, but little did I know he would mention the topic of nurse consulting a couple more times. It's like he was planting seeds, and before I knew it, I was giving more thought to the idea. It started to make sense. I already had a business administration degree with experience and I was in the process of obtaining my masters in nursing administration. Also, the way the business model was structured, I could incorporate my network of healthcare professionals and wellness advocates.

As I observed him execute his vision, connecting with others and building his strategy, I said to myself, "Hey…I'm going to jump on board also!" I was experiencing a small spark inside of me yet again and did not want to miss another opportunity. I felt I was on the brink of another change, and I gave myself permission to dream. We didn't know precisely how things would unfold, but we cautiously setup the vital components of operating a business and, before we knew it, we were a registered LLC company. My husband and I partnered together to create a company we were both passionate about! It was not easy and required much planning, but we stuck with it and the day finally came when our company, Walker Group The Consultants, LLC, had officially launched!

Dream Like No One Is Watching

As we worked to strategically build our business, my husband remained in his engineering position and I remained at the private practice. I also continuing working on my master's degree. Although working full time, operating a business and being a student required many late nights and extra work hours, it has been well worth the time invested. While I received encouragement from some to keep going, there were others who did not understand why we started our business and had many questions. I chose to not offer much attention to anyone not willing to understand my dream. After all, it's my dream!

My passion for helping, healing, giving, educating and advocating for others was exploding! I was now able to serve others in my own way, with a unique and tailored touch, while still operating within the nursing scope of practice. I eventually resigned from my private practice position to focus on completing my master's degree, and operating our business. I could not allow traditional, clinical status quo nursing to hinder me from living my idea of nursing, which is centered around my personality, as well as my passion for total wellness. To reach my nursing entrepreneurial dream, I had to remain disciplined and positive. I also learned to connect with others who are successfully practicing in the nurse entrepreneurial role for guidance.

Dreaming is now a part of the underlying rhythm to my life. It has centered me. Even with the presence of doubt and fear, visualizing where I desire to be, along with my spirituality, has led me to my end goal! I'm a stronger person and better nurse because of my choice to keep moving forward. I've given myself permission to be who I am - unapologetically!

Notions To Living Out Your Dreams:

1. Take time to find out who you really are. This will require alone time, prayer, meditation, list making, reminiscing about your past experiences; and maybe even counseling. Who are you? What are your passions?

2. Find out what you want out of life. Consider yourself and what truly makes you happy. Search your soul. Only you know your true desires.

3. Set goals for yourself. Keep positive images of your goals in front of you. Create a vision board if needed. Do whatever it takes to understand exactly where you're headed.

4. Establish a plan. Use a calendar and write out the steps to obtain your goals. Designate timelines. Be realistic, yet assertive.

5. Seek mentors and accountability partners. These individuals will not allow you to make excuses. They will be honest with you as you make decisions. They will have no ulterior motive.

6. Tailor your life's practices, habits, career choices, and daily decisions to your goals. Incorporate your personality to guarantee you are staying true to yourself.

7. Continue to learn. This may not involve obtaining another degree, but it does mean surrounding yourself with the knowledge you're seeking. Ask questions. Be eager to sharpen your skills and perfect your gifts.

8. Be confident. You know more than you think you do! Confidence will bring opportunities that sometimes knowledge cannot. Confidence is attractive.

9. Never stop dreaming! No matter how much fear may try to paralyze you while on your journey, keep going! People are

going to tell you your vision does not make sense, and some will even try to make you feel guilty for living out your dreams because of their own insecurities or inability to dream. None the less, keep dreaming! Remember, it's your dream!

10. Last, but certainly not least, keep God before you as you travel towards your dreams. He gives us the ability to dream, and provides the knowledge, strength and wisdom to reach our dreams. In all your ways, acknowledge Him and He will indeed direct your path!

Life Is But A Dream

Life. We all are a part of it, and we all desire to live it to the fullest. Arriving at the place of fulfillment and living our dreams commences when we allow ourselves to dream. Accept the journey. Believe and move towards it! Regardless of the situation into which we were born, or our upbringing, we all have the ability to choose. Let's make a conscious choice to keep dreaming!

Biography

Santisha's greatest passion is assisting others to live a balanced life and reach their full potential. She believes in an intentional and conscious approach to total wellness. After graduating from The University of North Carolina at Greensboro (UNCG) in 2005 with a Bachelor's of Science in Business Administration-Marketing and working in the Insurance Industry for 5 years, Santisha yearned to have a more profound impact on the health and personal lives of others, which led her to pursue a previous desire of becoming a nurse. She graduated with an Associate's Degree in Nursing from Wake Technical Community College (WTCC) in 2013. Santisha worked as a Cardiac nurse at WakeMed Hospital in Raleigh, North Carolina and then transitioned into Neurology at Raleigh Neurology Associates.

With a strong desire to move into a different facet of serving as a nurse, Santisha partnered with her husband as Co-Founder of Walker Group The Consultants, LLC, where she oversees the health sector, Walker Group Health & Wellness, as Senior Health Consultant. She shifted her focus to offering guidance, advocacy, and strategic and innovative solutions to healthcare consumers and providers. She manages the daily operations of the health sector while her team of health and wellness professionals provide safe, quality and effective health & wellness resolutions to companies, groups and organizations by way of educational seminars and workshops.

Shortly after launching Walker Group Health & Wellness, Santisha received her certification as a Wellness Coach from Spencer Institute; and the following year attained her Masters of Science in Nursing Administration degree from Gardner-Webb University (GWU).

In addition to total wellness, Santisha has a heart for the mental illness community, due to its effects on a close family member; and in 2014 partnered with her mother and sister as co-founder of Temple Vitality Foundation (TVF). TVF focuses on bringing awareness to mental illness and help transition this population to a state of independence through healthy living. She serves as TVF's Director of Marketing & PR and Medical Services.

Santisha adores inspiring others and has provided entrepreneurial and health-related inspiration in the community by way of public speaking at events, serving as a guest on local radio, as well as national and international nurse entrepreneurial and wellness podcasts. She is also an advocate for women empowerment by being a Contributing Author to the anthology Black Girls Hear, a Contributing Writing for the health section of the MizCEO Entrepreneurial Magazine, and serving as the Health & Wellness Instructor with Fierce Academy Online.

Santisha relishes in spending quality time with her best friend and husband of 10 years, she enjoys traveling, and welcomes the opportunity to meet new people. Santisha also understands the importance of taking time to replenish her own wellness tank, and appreciates moments of personal relaxation, meditation and prayer.

To connect with me for balanced living while obtaining your dreams:

www.santishawalker.com/www.walkergrouphw.com

FB: facebook.com/thebalancenursern

IG: Instagram.com/thebalancenurse.

Acknowledgments

First off, I would like to thank God for always making a way for me no matter what. Thank you to my husband, Harry Oldham IV, for just being you. Thank you to my mother and father for helping mold and shape me into the woman I am today. I would also like to give a special thanks to my children and niece for motivating me and being my "WHY". Thank you to the entire Manuel and Oldham family, for being my family. I am very thankful for the real life heroes that were present in my life. R.I.P to my grandmother Amelia G. Manuel, R.I.P Dorothy Raglin, and Joann Douglas. I hope and pray to be an inspiration to someone else, just as they have been to me. Also, thank you to my friend, patient, and mentor, Dr. Marcia Turner, for pushing me to stretch my wings. Thank you to Coach Michelle Rhodes, MHS, RN for being an example, that anything is possible, and inviting me on this venture. Special mentions: Alessi, Ica, Karvilla, Melissa, and my Diamond Diva sisters. I would like to dedicate this book to a man that always believed in me and loved me unconditionally; my grandfather, Dan Manuel.

Tasha

But God!

By Tasha Manuel Oldham, RN

It was an honor to work with such a well-accomplished group of ladies on this project. A group of true overcomers, dedicated to their causes; nurses and practitioners that are truly victorious women. I pray that this book inspires and motivates others in completing their goals in the medical profession. To empower the young people who're looking to pursue their dreams before life starts to twirl them around. That it encourages the person that has already started a family, and now finds herself juggling education and family commitments. I also hope that it gives support to those who think that age is a factor and that it may help you understand that your goals are attainable with hard work and determination. I pray that you will not be defeated by self -doubt, and naysayers that come to bring negative thoughts assisted by their lack of knowledge. Achieving your goals is the outcome of hard work and sheer perseverance. You have to know that you are going to make it. Say it to yourself until you are convinced.

I experienced many trials and tribulations throughout my journey to become a nurse. "Picture it, Cicely 1977," in my Sophia, from the Golden Girls, voice. Just kidding. Hope you have a sense of humor going into the medical profession.

While nursing can be gratifying, it can also be stressful - helping people through difficult times, whatever the diagnosis. It helps to have something about which to smile; it will keep your patience, as well as your mind, in a positive place. I must say that I'm so thankful for my victory. God has truly brought me over and out. I don't know what your faith is, but I pray you have some version of a higher power upon which to call. Each paragraph ends in my life references, "BUT GOD," for He is the source of everything.

Nursing is truly a ministry for me; it is something that I would honestly do for free if I were in better circumstances. I love helping others and trying to make their situations better; it is what I was put on this earth to do. For well over thirteen years, nursing has allowed me to work on my compassion for others, while being able to help support my family, leading me to my victory.

My first job, after graduating from high school, was working at Burlington Coat Factory in a retail position. I was enrolled in college classes but I wasn't taking it seriously because I was completely content in what I was doing. I had no real bills or responsibilities; just caring for myself. I would have at least three or four payroll checks before I would even take them to the bank to cash. I had no sense of urgency to finish school. I only enrolled and attended classes because it was what was expected of me after I graduated high school.

It wasn't until after the birth of my son that I truly wanted more. It was like night and day in my thinking; I realized that I had become a mother and I wanted a career that my son could be proud of his mom having. I had always wanted to be a nurse. I believed as a child that I had real-life heroes. I liked movie stars and musicians, just like all the other kids, but I never really wanted to be like them. One of my heroes was my Aunt Dot, a nurse who I admired and to whom I looked up. She was always well put together and was always able to take care of her family along with her job. My second hero was the mother of a childhood friend; she was a nurse as well. I can remember going to her job after school for a long time. Ms. Joann was her name, and she worked in the office of Dr. Metzgers. I had the opportunity to see nursing in two different settings. I can remember her interacting with patients; it was amazing. I recall seeing how much people depended on her; everyone with whom she came into contact held her in such high esteem. It was the nursing of both these women that formed my career path. My grandmother, Amelia G. Manuel, at one point was also enrolled in medical training classes, but she would choose her family over her career. Yet she took care of people as second nature. She never totally abandoned her caregiver ability, for she was a nurse to her family. Although she never wore the title, she truly was a nurse at heart.

These three women had such a powerful impact on my life, steering me into the nursing profession.

Motherhood was another thing that forced me to see the time that I had wasted, and I couldn't stay on that road anymore; I had no more time to waste. College seemed like it was just not moving fast enough for me - I was more of a hands-on type of person. I also harbored a fear of needles, but a talk with Ms. Joann worked out that issue. She told me that those who are scared of needles are the ones that end-up doing their best with people, making sure they only have to stick a patient once. I also got over the fear during my pregnancy. Because I was anemic, I had to have continuous blood work, which meant sticks upon sticks after sticks - every week at one point. I had eventually gotten over needles. I enrolled in the medical assistant course at Erwin Vocational Tech School, looking to start my journey in my chosen career. In technical school, the classes are hands-on, and I could have a career in only 1 year, which definitely sucked me in. There was a waiting list to get into the LPN class, but I was anxious to get into the medical field. I was impatient - I had a son to take care of now.

It was a strict process; nevertheless, I was determined that nothing would stop me. The teachers stayed on us like a drill sergeants in the military, weeding out people who were not serious. I didn't realize this at the time, because I was too young, and I hadn't taken school seriously. But there was no more time to slack off. I was on a mission. The teachers were violating people left and right. The teachers would remove all students that didn't take class and nursing seriously. It was like baseball; three strikes and you were out. I was determined that I wouldn't be the next victim. In my whole life, I had never been disrespectful toward an adult or someone that was an elder. I came every day, on time and in proper uniform, because I was not going to join the list of dropouts.

The course carried a lot of self-study, so you had to reach out to the instructors and that was not always well received. For me, at that moment, I politely expressed my need to successfully complete this course. I explained to them that I wasn't there to play. I was eager to learn and had a great spirit in everything I did. I had a son to support and a life to start living; therefore, my education was a part of my plan. Failure was not optional. My determination paid off and the hardest of instructors took me under her wing; she became one of my biggest encouragers. I grew to love the class that offered me 50% hands-on, which kept me engaged. My father kept my son for me while I worked and attended school.

The time passed quickly and I graduated in no time. I did my externship at Dr. Carthy and Dr. Rogals's office; eventually, I was hired for full-time employment upon completion of school. Sadly, when I took the certification for medical assistant, I did not pass. I was awarded the Diploma, yet I was extremely devastated by my results. I felt that I was knowledgeable on the material. At least I thought I was; the test really didn't seem that hard. The certification wasn't needed for the medical assistant field; you were paid the same at most places at the time, whether you had it or not. So, I decided that I wouldn't try to test again.

I loved the profession! I worked in the same office for 5 years. I enjoyed helping people and soon what became my passion was drawing blood, especially from the difficult patients. I loved the challenge. I met a lot of well-accomplished people. I was always ready to learn new things. It was a great feeling and I was content with my work - until I gave birth to my second child. It was shortly thereafter that I desired to move upward and accepting that I was no longer content.

I was in full understanding that, monetarily, I would need more than what I presently brought home. The truth was, I was operating as a single-parent. My husband and father of my children decided to take a vacation from his responsibilities, making me the sole support of our two children. I continued to press forward. Knowing it would not be long before my situation would tackle me down, I quickly enrolled back at Erwin and was placed on the waiting list. I would check the list daily, and found myself quickly moving up.

I had just happened to be calling that day to check my status on the list when the opportunity opened; God opened the doors that I needed. I was working in the Doctor's office, trying to maintain both my personal and professional life. I had a husband, two children to take care of, my career, and now school. I was seriously juggling and wearing many hats. I did, thankfully, have the help of my father and grandfather, who helped me with the kids. Even still, it was hard. That is why I try to encourage young people not to waste time; start working on your goals right away. It wasn't too late for me though; I had this life to maintain and I was determined to do the best that I could possibly do for my children. Many times, I wanted to give up, but my children helped keep me motivated; I wasn't doing it for me - I was doing it for them. Their little faces pushed me like no tomorrow. I went to school every day, but it wasn't anything like the previous medical assistant course - it was 10 times worse. They made sure you would quit if you were not serious. But like I said before, quitting wasn't an option for me; I had to push through. With hard work and study groups, I made it through.

Once I graduated, I was terrified to take the boards for my LPN, since I failed the medical assistant certification before. I studied and put it off until one of my classmates convinced me to move the date up. She boosted my confidence up to a 10; I had been well trained and studied. You have to rely on everything you've learned and use your nursing judgement to pick the correct answer. As I was taking the test, the computer shut off; I believe I had answered only 80 questions. It shocked me because I was told it could go over 200 questions. I was terrified it could have meant I did very good…or very bad. I immediately tried to look up questions that I had on the test, to try and determine if I had gotten them right, but I couldn't remember very much afterward. I finally just decided to relax about it and wait. Soon, I learned that I had passed and it was at that very moment I started recalling questions from the medical assistant certification that I had failed years ago. Recalling choices - and my answers - just like it happened yesterday, was something that remained consistent as I was recalling the questions and my answers. It clicked just like that - I was answering as a nurse on a medical assistant test. The majority of the answers were to be reported to the nurse in some form or fashion. God spoke to me at that very moment that this was my destiny…I was meant to be a nurse…had I passed that test it would have prolonged my goal of becoming a nurse because I would have been content as a medical assistant and that is not what I wanted to be. Tears of joy came scrolling down my face. It was at that moment I learned to be just as thankful for my failures as I am for my victories, because every time it has been for my good. Every time it has worked out and something greater came and it is at that moment I understand why it had to be that way for me.

Soon after I passed my boards, I decided to pursue a career at the hospital to gain more experience. I hated leaving all the patients and all my old coworkers - "the gang" – the MA's, the nurse practitioners and the doctors. We had been like a small family, so it was bitter sweet. With all the experience and knowledge I learned while working for a cardiologist, I had no problem getting in the door. I got hired on a progressive care unit/telemetry floor. I worked a year, gaining knowledge daily. I was working as an LPN. Though I didn't care at the time, I knew that one day the contentment would wear off, so I started taking my prerequisites for my RN - one at a time - since I wasn't in a rush.

Soon, I wanted to become an RN and I began researching programs. I discovered a school that allowed you to start nursing classes while you were completing your prerequisites. This type of program was well within my plans. It was the school I needed. The main hurdle with which I had to deal was the distance to the school. It was quite a distance to attend daily, but the local school had a huge waiting list and you had to be finished with your prerequisites, which was out for me. I needed to get started towards my goal right away. I had a sense of urgency, so I enrolled.

Everything was going great with school; however, my life outside of school started becoming very challenging, which started mentally draining me. My mother-in-law ended up moving in with us, and she was a major help for me – with the kids and around the house. We also got along well. I will always be grateful to have had her. I was also helping my grandparents, running a house, kids, trying to work on my marriage - all while working a full-time job. To say the least, it was a handful. Additionally, my grandpa's health started to fail, I found out I had another baby on the way and I was paddling to stay afloat. I was on my feet at work and on my feet at clinicals…it became a lot for my body! But I only had a little longer to go. I had to push through. I ended up failing a class by one point.

Another set-back: I ended up having my baby two and a half months early. She was less than two pounds. Had I not failed that one class by one point, I would have been about done with school. I was getting down on myself but there was no time; I had a baby girl that was fighting for her life. She was with a pod of babies, three of whom died while she was there - one on the right, one on the left and one in front. It was all too real. I knew that I wouldn't be able to handle the loss of my child. I prayed for those parents and what they were going through. The baby in front of us had all kinds of religious people coming in and praying for him. When God called him home, it really hit home. Layani had a mother that was falling apart, a father that wasn't doing much better, a grandmother that was praying faithfully everyday with her prayer sisters. On the phone, we had family and church family, but nothing like this other baby had at the hospital. After talking with a stranger at the hospital - I couldn't tell you if it was a visitor or a staff member to this day - but after talking to him, I had faith that my baby would make it, and a lady from pastoral care came and gave me another confirmation. We decided on her name right then. Sister Murray, the mother of my church, said something that resonated with me, and I knew that Layani would make it. Most of the time, even people of faith tell you that God's will be done, but all three of these people said something similar, something that gave me a "yes" when no one else could.

I started back at school to finish where I left off, which turned out to be a blessing because one of my teachers was an expert. After talking to her, I saved my baby from unnecessary testing that was dangerous to undergo because she was so small. Had it not been for my teacher, Ms. Lane, I would not have been knowledgeable enough to question orders for my baby and unnecessary tests that weren't going to change her treatment. Some doctors were upset with me because I wasn't just going along with everything without reasoning behind it. Others responded with kindness and answers to my questions. It worked out for the good of my child. After 2 and a half months, she was able to come home. Still, my life was like a roller coaster. My grandpa's heart failure was worse. I was helping him with this, while also being a mother for the third time, trying to hang on as a wife, a full time employee and a student. I don't know how I did it...but God.

I graduated, took my boards right away and passed! Victory was won! Through your journey, you have to make up in your mind that you are going to push through - no matter what. My grandpa made it until after I graduated and Layani was home awhile. He was so proud, which was the victory for me. I continued my nursing career at the hospital for thirteen more years. Now I have begun a career as an RN case manager, dealing with end-of-life care. Another new journey and challenge. My best advice is to keep the faith that you will make it and push through, and use birth control (smile). Nursing has been so rewarding for me! I truly am glad that I pushed through and I pray that you do, too, no matter what life throws your way.

Biography

I pray that this book blesses you and brings you encouragement. It is my hope that it will be a light to someone. A little about me, my name is Tasha Manuel Oldham. I am married to a hard-working husband. I have 3 beautiful biological children and 4 beautiful bonus children. I'm a native of Tampa, Florida. Nursing is truly a ministry for me, I believe I was called to be a nurse by God. It gives me great joy to help others. It has been a long road for me, I started out as an medical assistant and I served in a local doctor's office for over five years until I graduated as a Licensed Practical Nurse from Erwin Technical Center then went to serve at St Joseph's Hospital as a staff nurse. After working a couple of years there, I started working toward my goal of becoming a registered nurse. I graduated from Galen school of nursing in 2008 and continued my career as an RN at St Joseph's until 2016. Currently, I work as a hospice RN case-manager; providing care for adults and children suffering with life-limiting illnesses. I continue to serve in the community to make it a better place through organizations such as Black Nurses Rock, where I have met Nurses with a strong drive and determination such as Michelle Rhodes, MHS, RN who is making it possible for many Nurses to become more effective in the community as well as entrepreneurs. I serve on the board of the Tampa Diamond Divaz, yes with a z on the end. It is a sassy ladies social group as well as a community service group that works together all over the Tampa Bay Area to help make it a better place. I am also co-founder of Anchorage Ministries, along with Dr. Marcia Turner, that strives to spread love to all.

Acknowledgments

I would like to thank God for his continued mercy and grace on my life, I am nothing without you God. To my Husband Mikal Aziz, I love you more than you will ever know, thank you for always supporting me and to my 5 children, everything I sacrificed was for you all to have a better life, I love you with every fiber of my being!

Nefertiti

Life Happened Along the Way

By Nefertiti Aziz, BSN, RN

Early in my life, helping people was something I knew I wanted to do. Even as a child, I couldn't stand to see someone cry or be sad. It would just break my heart that there was nothing I could do to help them or make them feel better.

My life was uneventful for most of my childhood up until the age of 16, which, to say the very least, was when life started happening to me. On November 13, 2000, I was walking home from band practice after school when a man pulled into a driveway I was about to cross. He was driving a dark green 4 door sedan and I thought this was his residence, so I stopped to let him pull into his carport. However, little did I know this was not his home. Instead, this man got out of his car with a gun in his hand, pointed it at my face and told me to get in the car. I didn't know what to do; I froze and, scared for my life, I complied with his request and got in the car. After about a 10-minute drive, we arrived at his house, where he proceeded to rape me for about an hour and a half. After the assault, he apologized and asked if there was somewhere I needed to be dropped off and he begged me not to tell anyone. I assured him that I wouldn't tell a soul and, as soon as he opened the side door to his house, I took off running to my boyfriend's house, which was close by. His mom called my mom and she explained what happened to me. My mom arrived shortly after my boyfriend's mom hung up and took me to the hospital.

While at the hospital, the staff ran a battery of tests and detectives asked me a lot of questions and all I wanted to do was go home, shower and go to sleep. But little did I know that my life was about to change forever. The nurse came back in the room where my mom, Aunt, boyfriend and I were waiting and said, "Ms. Fleming, I have one of your test results back, I'm sorry but you're pregnant!!!!" "Wait, what…what do you mean I'm pregnant? I only had sex twice, 2 months ago, with my boyfriend AND my period just went off, like, last week!" I yelled, in shock, at the nurse. My mom yelled, "Oh No!" my Aunt's mouth was wide open, and my boyfriend was called out of the room by the detective. I sat there on that hospital bed in silence, shocked. I could not speak; nurses and doctors were talking to me, asking me questions, but all I saw was their mouths moving. I heard them, but not really; I couldn't focus on anything. The only thing that kept playing in my head was scenes of this strange man on top of me, smelling strongly of alcohol and with a gun to my head, with porn playing loudly in the background and this nurse was telling me that I was pregnant.

Hours passed before the nurse came in and softly said, "I need to perform a rape kit." I looked at her as I spread my legs apart as wide as I could and said, fighting back tears, "at this point you can have your way as well; I have already been humiliated and violated, so it doesn't matter." She looked at me with such pity in her eyes and said, "I am so sorry." The nurse took all my clothes, samples of my pubic hair and performed a vaginal exam. After she was finished, I was finally allowed to go home. That car ride was one of the longest rides ever - no one said a word the whole way home. I did not go to school for about a week, but when I did return, I was bombarded with questions from the other students and, needless to say, I was not in the mood to answer any of them.

After I returned home from my first day back, I was met in my yard by the detectives and was asked to come to the station for some additional questions. I told them I would let my mom know so she could bring me when she gets off from work. The next day, my mom and I arrived at the station, and the detective had my mom wait up front, which I thought was odd. I arrived at the interrogation room and entered, followed by a detective. As soon as I sat down, she started yelling at me, saying, "Why are you lying about this innocent man? You know you wanted to have sex with him!" I was in shock, scared and pissed all at the same time. I started crying and yelled at her, "Why would I lie about something like that, I don't even know this man; never seen him in my life!" She looked at me with a snarky grin and said, "You're pregnant, right? So I am guessing you lied to try to cover up the pregnancy so you wouldn't get in trouble with your parents, but you didn't think we were going to give you a pregnancy test, huh?" That's when I realized I was pregnant. I had totally forgotten about that - with the rape and then going back to school - I forgot I was pregnant. I started crying uncontrollably at this point and, when I composed myself, I took on the anger of a thousand slaves from my ancestral tree and I cussed (not cursed) this white detective out, calling her all kinds of names and demanding she tell me why I would do something like that. After she unclutched her pearls, she explained to me that they let this man go and they were considering pressing charges against me for filing a false police report. I got up cussed her out some more, told her they knew where to find me and I left the room. Crying, I ran to my mom but, oddly enough, she didn't ask me what happened.

We got in the car and I noticed we were not going in the direction of our house; instead, we arrived at a doctor's office. So, I'm thinking, "Okay, since I'm pregnant, I'm here to be seen." After about a 15-minute wait, we got a call back to an office, not an exam room, and I'm thinking to myself, "Umm…okay…where is the exam table?" I looked over at my mom and she had this look on her face like she had an attitude. After about 5 minutes of waiting, in walked a tall, medium-built African American man. He walked around his desk, sat down and said, "Hello, Ms. Fleming, my name is Dr. XYZ and I'm a CHILD PSYCHOLOGIST." I sat there looking dumb founded, like maybe I was hearing things. He started talking about something, but I was still stuck on the child psychologist part. He called my name abruptly, which made me snap out of the land of what-the-hell-is-going-on and asked me how long I had been promiscuous. I did not reply to him at first because I was thinking to myself, "Did he just call me a Hoe?" He chuckled and said, "Ms. Fleming, do you know what that means?" I looked at him right through his glasses and said, "YES, it means being a HOE!!!" Before he could respond, I turned my head like the little girl from the Exorcist toward my mom and in a calm voice, looking her in her eyes, said "Bitch, have you lost your fucking mind?"

I didn't even give her a chance to react. I got up and left the building. From that day on, I was no longer the quiet, sweet, non-cursing Nefertiti everyone knew and loved. That girl died that day. I was now Nefertiti, who only wore hoodies, so no one could tell what gender I was so I wouldn't get raped again. I was now the girl at school who lied about being raped because my mom talked to the counselors, who talked to the teachers, who told their kids who attended the high school and that's why I had to drop out of school in the eleventh grade. I was being talked about and teased every day. I could not believe no one believed me just because I was pregnant. I mean okay - I did get a little hot in the pants and had sex twice with my boyfriend - but that did not justify the backlash I received. I was hurt! The one thing that did not change was I never stopped going to church. My Pastor, Apostle Brenda Howard and the amazing women of House of prayer Christian Fellowship (now known as Tabernacle of Prayer Christian Fellowship) kept me covered in prayer and made sure I never gave up on God and for that I am FOREVER grateful.

After dropping out of school, I enrolled in the teen parenting center to try to get my high school diploma, but at this point, I was mad at the world and I made sure everyone knew it! I became a teenager on a rampage, walking the streets, at 2am – 3am, to clear my head, not caring if I got raped again. I mean, I lived through the first time I got raped, right? I had my first child on July 27th, 2001 - a beautiful baby girl - and I promised her on that day that I would protect her with everything that was in me. The following December, I came home from school and went straight to my room as I always did, but when I opened my door, I noticed all my things were gone - I mean everything - my baby clothes, my bed, my clothes…everything. There was no trace of me or my baby ever staying there. I called my mom and went off on her. After my verbal assault was finished, she told me I was being kicked out and my stuff was at my older sister's house. After a short stay with my older sister, I found myself with a five-month-old at the Salvation

Army shelter for the homeless. So, I made the decision that I was on my own and I needed to help myself.

I dropped out of the parenting center, obtained my GED and got a job. After being at the Salvation Army shelter for seven months, I was allowed to get emergency section 8, since I was almost 18 years old. After I received my housing and food stamps, things started to turn in my favor. My daughter's father moved in with me and that relationship became very abusive for 4 years. In those 4 years, my birth control shot failed and I had another child on March 2, 2004 - a son - at nineteen years old. So, with 2 kids and a sorry, leaching boyfriend (who I loved very much and about whom I would fight anybody who said anything wrong), I made life work as best as I could.

A year later, I made up my mind to become a Registered Nurse. One day, I ran into the valedictorian of my graduating class from high school. We had short talk and I asked her if she was taking any college classes. She explained to me that she was attending the state college to get her Bachelor of Science in Nursing but that she had flunked out. I was devastated. I thought to myself, if the valedictorian couldn't become a nurse, how could I, with my little raggedy GED? That was the biggest mistake I could have made. I let someone else's failure dictate my future. So, for the next year, I found myself trying to figure out what I wanted to do with my life - with school, my kids and the very abusive relationship in which I found myself in.

Then, on September 2, 2005, I was driving in the middle of nowhere and my entire wheel popped off my car, which made it slowly roll to a stop in front of the only decent looking house on the street. I did not have a cell phone, so I got out of my car and sat on the porch of this stranger's house until the owner came home. And that's when I met my knight in shining armor, my breath of fresh air and my now husband, Mikal Aziz. Mikal let me stay the night in his bed while he slept on the couch. I still had the mindset that I survived being raped before, so it couldn't be that bad if it happened again, so I slept peacefully in his bed that night. The next morning, he went to work and one of his friends came with a cell phone for me to use. I called my boyfriend to come and get me, but when he arrived, he beat me with a wrench on my back and head because he was upset I didn't come home. Luckily, someone down the street saw what was happening, called the police and pulled him off me. My boyfriend left before the police arrived. Shortly after the incident, Mikal arrived home from work, saw my injuries and has never left my side since that day.

Fast forward eight months to Mother's Day, May 14, 2006. I received a phone call from a familiar voice. It was my dad, whom I hadn't spoken to in 9 months. We had the best conversation ever! We caught up on the time that was lost, and I gave him one of my older sister's phone number so he could call her. Four days later, on May 18, 2006, somewhere around 11p.m, I received a call from my oldest sister. She was hysterical; screaming through the phone so that I could barely understand her. "Slow down, wait…what? SLOW DOWN, WAIT… WHAT? DADDY HAS BEEN WHAT?" I screamed back at her. She finally calmed down and said, "Daddy has been shot! Our brother shot daddy!" Nah, that's not what I heard; what do you mean? I just talked to the both of them, like, four days ago, I thought to myself. That was the longest night of my life. See, you have to understand that my daddy may have been an abusive husband and an alcoholic, but he was still my daddy. The times that he was around us sober he was the best dad a girl could have wanted.

On May 20th, I called to check on my dad in the ICU in Mississippi; he was awake, and we talked. He sounded weak and after every word he said, "I love you." I was confused as to why he kept saying I love you but I really didn't stress the issue. My dad told me he was feeling better and I didn't need to rush to see him. I told him okay and I would be there in the next couple of days. Little did I know that would be the last time I would ever talk to him. On Monday, May 22, 2006, he succumbed to his injuries. My world had just been turned upside down and a part of my heart died and is still dead. I would later go on to find out that my oldest brother shot my daddy once in the side and twice in the back. Looking back on our last conversation, I think my dad knew it would be our last.

After coming home from the funeral, I enrolled in to the local community college to become a surgical tech. During this time, my birth control failed again (yes, again) and I became pregnant with another son, who was born on May 6th, 2007. I graduated and moved to Florida with Mikal and our three kids. In 2008, I decided I was going to finally give nursing a try, so I went to one of the local for-profit schools and took the entrance exam and I FAILED by 2 points. So, I gave up another big mistake and birth control failed AGAIN. I asked the doctor what on earth was going on? He told me I just fell into that 1% for whom birth control does not work. I had another daughter on November 28, 2008.

Soon after her birth I got a job in housekeeping at a local hospital and was content in my new position - or so I thought. Six months went by and I started feeling like I could do better; that this was not what was meant for me. So, I attended church the next Sunday and planted a seed offering and went to take my nursing entrance exam again. This time I passed the entrance exam by 1 point and so, in 2009, I started school.

Going to school with 4 kids, a full time job and a marriage was hard. I transferred to a CNA position with the same hospital, working three 12 hour night shifts. So, I was working three 12 hr. night shifts, getting off work at 7am, going straight to school, staying at school until 4pm, taking a nap in the car, showering in the OR locker room and going back to work. I had to tell my husband (a lot) "I promise I am not cheating on you, please don't leave, just hang in there, it will all pay off in the end."

Then my life took another blow. In May 2011, I was at work and I started to have trouble seeing and I had a little bit of slurred speech that came and went in a couple of seconds; it also happened again the next day on my way to school. I got concerned and drove myself to the hospital. I was admitted and diagnosed with Multiple Sclerosis (MS). After I was released from the hospital, I didn't have time to process what I was just told - I had to finish school. The stress of being sick, working, being a mom and wife took a toll on my relationship with my husband and we eventually ended up in marriage counseling to save our marriage and it was the best investment ever.

Around December 2011, I noticed the string for my Marina IUD was a little longer than usual so I decided to get it checked to make sure it was still in place. The doctor walked in smiling and shaking his head, so I'm thinking. "Okay, cool…him shaking his head means I'm good. He is probably wondering how on earth I knocked this thing out of place and I have to explain that one night we got drunk last month." So the doctor sat down in front of me and said, " Mrs. Aziz, the bad news is you did knock the IUD out of place but the good news is I can put it back in place but you have to wait seven months," and he started smiling. Me, not catching on quick enough, asked, "Why seven months? Can't we get this done today, like, right now?" He started laughing and I was still sitting there looking slow, like, what is your problem? Then it hit me, and I screamed, "WAIT, I'M PREGNANT!!" The doctor said yes, and I immediately started crying, saying, "I only have 7 more months in school."

So, now I am working three 12hr day shifts, pregnant, going to school and clinicals, trying to be a good wife, trying to be a good mother and studying - all at the same time. I went into pre-term labor twice, but I gradated on June 12th, 2012 - pregnant. I cried a lot that day, I was so proud of myself. I had been through so much in life and I could not believe I made it with my sanity and still married. On July 15, 2012 I had a son via emergency C-section due to a prolapsed cord and on August 29th I sat for the NCLEX and passed.

With this journey to becoming a nurse, I have learned that all my life experiences individually were horrible but, collectively, they showed me how strong I could be and how much God loved me. I have learned to not let other people's failures dictate my future successes and that you have to know who you are. Know that you are stronger than what your situation is making you feel like at that point in time. Never give up, no matter what! You do not have to be a product of your environment. You do not have to become a statistic. Okay, you messed up – fine. Cry about it and then get passed it but never forget it so you will not make the same mistake again. Be your own cheerleader and find something that motivates you to keep pushing. I used to ride through the "rich" neighborhood and pick out a beautiful house and tell myself, "Soon, soon this will be you. Just keep going!" and when I felt like quitting, I would drive to "my house" to remind myself of my goals. I did that for 2 yrs. (I'm surprised I didn't get the cops called on me riding past this house so much). Know who you are in God and claim what's rightfully yours, it's out there waiting for you with your name on it!

"All hard work brings a profit, but mere talk leads only to poverty." (Proverbs 14:23, NIV)

Biography

Despite many obstacles in her life Nefertiti Aziz has rose above them all to achieve her goals. As a nursing student struggling in life, she earned the "Distinguished Graduate" award for her graduating class at Breckenridge School of Nursing. Nefertiti went on to receive her BSN from Western Governors University and has now been a critical care nurse for 5 years where she has received multiple Customer Service Awards. Even with all her accomplishments Nefertiti does not plan to stop here, and she hopes her story will inspire and encourage anyone entering the nursing field or facing any type of adversity while trying to achieve their goals.

Acknowledgements

My contributing chapter is based on the victorious accomplishments, and storms battled throughout a season of a divorce and academic achievement. The kindest regards go out to Michelle Rhodes for creating this platform for future authors and accepting my participation. I am grateful for my family and friends who supported my daughters and me. A special thank you to Northwest Louisiana Technical College Mansfield for the prompt enrollment assistance and fantastic financial student services. Thanks also to the dedicated nursing department and instructors who never give up on me and continued to inspire my best. Nursing school is not successfully achieved alone and with a valuable study group of my fellow classmates: Jackie, Yashika, and Freida; I was able to graduate. It takes a village to raise a child and Temple of Knowledge Church and Christian Academy exemplified love and support, my daughters, and I would like to thank each and everyone. Finally, I would like to thank my daughters Klaudia and Kriscilla for navigating through a difficult time, and I love both of you very much.

Latarsia

Overcoming Victoriously

By Latarsia WyKeela Maxie, LPN

Life can change in an instant. Sometimes we treat our lives as if they were these fixed structures that are constant as long as we build them with that intent. Like, if we build a marriage and a home and a family and household, then because we did the best we could, that should mean that's a stable structure to rely upon. I mean, the house we live in feels permanent enough…the people around us seem like they'll always be there because we can't seem to get away from them…and it looks like we'll still be able to turn on "Good Morning America" and sip hot chocolate out of the same mug every morning. But life isn't that way as much as we trick ourselves into believing.

Most of us measure success by what we have and what we can present to the world. It doesn't sound flattering, but it's understandable. We're visual creatures, so we have evolved to be able to identify success at a glance. But over the past few years, I learned the true formula for success, and it involves nothing you can see with just your eyes.

It is only when something happens to destroy the status quo that we see the truth about how ephemeral everything really is. It's then that we learn what success really is and how to actually obtain it.

Life took a rapid turn one early fall morning in Washington State. I had a weird feeling in the pit of my stomach for a while. Some like to call it, "women's intuition." With a full day of routines awaiting me, the phone rang, and I was totally unprepared for what I was about to hear.

My girl's father and then husband's voice was short and clipped on the other end; he sounded unlike himself and immensely familiar - all at the same time. His words were slow and careful, and then all of a sudden rushed and defensive, and even a bit defiant. Someone was pregnant, and he was the reason. It was definitely confirmation that my marriage was over.

I went numb for the first time after wondering how exactly that feels. Now I knew. Not only did I just find out that he was cheating again, but she was actually pregnant. I had so many questions. What about the girls – our children? What do I tell them? What about me? Where and how do I start divorce proceedings? With family living over 2,000 miles away in the south, how do maintain and raise my kids? Do I move and leave my newly built house? Or do I remain in the area I called home for the past six years? His baby was growing inside of someone else while his daughters were growing outside every day, marking their heights on the bathroom doorway. Not to mention that, as a military officer, he was in danger of being kicked out for violating the code of conduct. This was a pure disaster.

I told him to move and not to bother coming back. I remember the finality of hanging up that phone vividly. As the connection was cut, I felt an invisible slice go through me as I thought about my entire life…I needed a plan…and quick!

After three phone calls to the police (due to heightened arguments), I packed everything in my Camry Hybrid and moved my girls and me from Washington State to Louisiana. I left my house, my way of life and everything behind. We moved in with my parents in the town in which I grew up. On the drive, I envisioned my estranged husband walking into an empty house and secretly hoped that it might feel even a little like what I felt on the phone. But I knew it was a pointless desire. He already had the makings of a brand new life in place - another family already started and ready to go. Conversely, I was starting from scratch.

When I arrived in Louisiana, I knew I wanted to feel like I had more of a plan that I really had. As I searched for another job in my field of expertise, I filled my time with three jobs. As my cousins were getting ready to go to nursing school, I joined them thinking this would help fill my time until I found an IT job. I was easily able to get my transcripts pushed through and was able to start quickly. I felt a little bit relieved knowing that I was working toward something.

The best part of nursing school was that it was just down the street from my daughters' school, so the logistics worked out, and I was close by. But that's where the easy conveniences stopped. Nursing school was intense. It was more difficult than I anticipated, especially since I breezed through my IT degree with such ease. Nursing school was my saving grace and the restoration of my relationship with God. I had become very angry with God for allowing my marriage to fail after working so diligently and praying throughout the years.

I was overcome with anger. And I was especially angry at God for my circumstances. It seemed like there was always some unfair predicament turning up whenever things started to look good.

After successfully finishing my Information Technology degree with honors. I was invited by Columbia University to apply to their school. But I never uprooted and attended, as I placed my family as the priority.

Nursing school was a humbling experience because it wasn't where my natural strength was, but that didn't mean it was impossible. It simply meant I had to faithfully work for it if I wanted it.

Things outside of school were hard, too, but it's adversity that cultivates the strongest characters. My girls and I made sacrifices, but we got through it. We lived in a tiny bedroom, slept on bunk beds and commuted at ungodly hours to get where we needed to be on time. The thing that kept me going and able to inspire my girls to keep going as well was that I knew that this was not an ending. We were in transition, and it was tough, but with a little perseverance and faith, we'd come out stronger than how we went in.

What you see when you leave the safety of a nuclear family existence and start trying to make it as a single parent is how important your network is. The people who show up to help you, when you feel at your worst, are an unbelievable miracle. I can't explain these people or their generosity of time and spirit other than as a gift and blessing from God.

The local children's librarian used to watch and help feed my kids as I studied for hours. The janitor of the school constantly offered his prayers, and the girls' teachers and administrators were helpful in every way. I truly believe in the expression, "It takes a village," and I don't think I could've done what I've done without these small acts of kindness. And, in retrospect, they aren't small at all, they are blessings from God.

After lots of hard work, I passed nursing school, and my state boards, the first time. I also was blessed enough to rekindle my relationship with my high school sweetheart. It had been circumstances that kept us apart, and now it was circumstances that brought us back together. Today, we are happily married. I am a Licensed Practical Nurse looking to merge my two expertise, Information Technology, and nursing, in the emerging Informatics Nursing field.

What I know now is that success cannot be measured by what you have. It's too precarious, and any of what we have can be taken away at any moment. But there is something that cannot be taken away, and that is the true measure of success. If you have faith and perseverance, you can always recreate whatever gets lost - because you will always have the tools within to rebuild. My ex-husband didn't take anything away from me that early fall morning. Instead, he revealed an opportunity for me to look within myself, dust off my work boots and watch the magic that happens when faith and hard work merge.

From this point on, I know anything can be taken from me, but circumstances can never shatter me because my success is defined by a metric that only I can touch. The metric of success is a lot like having a cloud backup. Every system can break; everything you have built can be lost. But if you have faith and perseverance in your cloud backup, you have all the tools you need to be successful - regardless of what comes your way. Many blessings to all!

Biography

LaTarsia WyKeela Maxie is a Licensed Practical Nurse and a Summa Cum Laude graduate in Computer Networking Security Systems with concentrations in Microsoft Network Administration & Security, Network Security, Firewall and Detection Systems, and Computer & Communication Security. She is gifted with a dual analytical-creative mind, which is itself bolstered by her outstanding interpersonal, leadership, and organizational abilities. Whether she is leading a team or playing her role in one, the high quality of her work is sure to stand out.

For more than twenty years, she has volunteered and sacrificed her time throughout various organizations and communities. Latarsia is Co-Leader of Hiring Our Heros Military Spouse Professional Network Hampton Roads Virginia, Founder of Black Nurses Rock Hampton Roads Virginia Chapter, Inc., Advisor of Hampton Roads Chief Petty Officer Spouse Association, and a Member of the Steering Committee of Continuum Resource of Education. Additionally, as a full-time nursing student at Tidewater Community College, she has aspirations of furthering her education to Master of Science in Nursing - Informatics. Latarsia resides in Virginia Beach, VA with her husband Patrick and four kids.

Acknowledgements

It would be remiss to not acknowledge my Lord and Saviour, Jesus Christ, for always being by my side and guiding me to my life's purpose. I dedicate this book to You, and pray it accomplishes Your will.

I love you, Lord! I am forever grateful for ALL things.

I would like to thank my husband, Reggett, for hanging in there, and allowing me to follow my dreams.

Thank you to my four beautiful children. Jasmine, Rashad, Jayden, and Chance, you are the reason I push myself. I pray you are proud of your mommy, and I inspire each of you to follow your own path and accomplish your dreams.

This is my public acknowledgement to all my family and friends who supported me during my nursing education. The love and patience shown to me and my family is greatly appreciated.

Raven

Purposed to Win: A Victorious Nurse Anthology

By Raven Little, RN-BC

What We Hold

It's interesting what we hold onto in our lives. We sometimes delude ourselves into thinking we hold onto only the good and what makes us better or stronger. We pride ourselves on how we know what's best for our bodies, our minds and our spirits. We tell ourselves that we know our limits, what our goals should be and we're doing the best we can with what we have.

Except every so often, what we unknowingly hold onto the tightest are the painful things - the shortcomings, the disappointments and the unhappiness. We hold onto so much of what's bad and unhealthy, that there's often no room for what's good. Oftentimes, we disregard our connection to the One who gave us our drive and determination and rely on that inner voice of independence because we believe we know what is best for us. We overlook those subtle signs from God, or that gentle nudge from the Holy Spirit, attempting to guide us along the correct path. We cling to our pain because we think that doing so, in such trying times in our lives, is a clear indication of our strength. And we fail to realize that, quite possibly, it requires more strength…or rather, more faith…to let go of all this detritus weighing us down than it is to hold onto it.

Consequently, we banish our hopes and dreams to a vision board set on a corner of our desk, at a job that we hate because it seems like earning an income at any cost is the most important thing. We need to make ends meet and keep the dangers at bay. But this type of self-fulfilling cycle that is centered on maintaining our immediate needs sometimes ends up working against us. Because it's the bigger goals, the more perilous dreams and the uncertain endeavors, that procure more satisfying, more rewarding results. But these are easy to push off to another day because usually what seems most important are the bills currently in the mailbox and the immediate needs of our family.

And sometimes, we're so miserable at our job that even that little vision board starts to mock us, sitting there showing us all the amazing things that others have but we don't. The longer we stare at the pictures of other nurses, the stethoscopes around other people's necks, the nice home, vacations and other aspirations, we start to believe that some dreams never come true, and we wonder, with trepidation, if ours fall into that category. We wonder if our prayers are being heard and begin to question our purpose in life. Some days we can find nothing but resentment for that vision board, and so we cling even tighter to the things we don't even want in the first place.

That's where I was in 2010. I was clinging to a customer service job that depleted my spirit and exhausted my soul. I trudged into work every single day, but I didn't like what I was doing - at all. During my thirty-minute commute to work, it was imperative that I listen to some of the gospel greats, such as Yolanda Adams or Kirk Franklin, just to keep my sanity and face my work day. A constant thought throughout my day was how I was wasting eight hours of my life, five days per week, without some type of self-fulfillment or benefit to my family and community. Yes, I brought home a paycheck that supported my three children, but the job didn't bring me any joy. It didn't light me up. It didn't inspire me. And it didn't give me the ability to help people in the way I so craved and knew was part of my life's purpose.

My co-workers, mentors and managers knew I was unhappy at my job. Whenever anyone came over to me during work, I'd notice their eyes move across my vision board. They saw photos of nurses and dreams of owning a business rather than goals of providing stellar customer service. During one-on-one quality coaching sessions, my mentor would coach me on accomplishing my health care career goals, and the focus was hardly ever on improving my customer service skills. Over the years, I lost that twinkle in my eye. The sadness and lack of motivation was noticeable, but yet, I was too fearful to trust my heart and leave what I thought was security. It was more comfortable for me to stay. Or so I thought.

What We Believe

As I look back to such a painful time in my life, I recall one of my favorite Bible scriptures that was central to my vision board. "For I know the plans I have for you," declares the Lord, "plans to prosper you and not to harm you, plans to give you hope and a future." (Jeremiah 29:11). Talk about contradictory. I knew my life was purposed for so much more, but my actions did not match my beliefs. I was still operating and living my life from a point of complacency and fear. This was NOT the plan God had for me.

Nonetheless, Jeremiah 29:11 was a vital mantra for me in those days. It was my anchor. It was my rock. It was sanity. Every shift at my customer service job, I had to remind myself that God had GOOD plans for me, and that although those included this job at the time, it didn't mean that this job was the final destination. It was a means to an end, a paycheck to a better life, somehow…at some point.

But as my husband often says about me, "I hold on to things for too long." In retrospect, I can see how this is exactly true. I was holding on to this particular job because it seemed like it was part of the plan. And the fact that it was such a struggle to get through each day meant I was building up faith and strength for something wonderful and miraculous to happen. And that might be true to an extent, but eventually, it started to get in the way of my dream and was no longer fueling the bigger goal. I was living paycheck to paycheck, I was exhausted from working and raising a family and I was disenchanted with life. This job had started to feel like an end rather than the means to an end, which is probably why I was so fed up.

The Turning Point

My frustration eventually materialized into an unacceptable call with a customer, but at this point I was beyond caring. I knew I was being recorded and would probably be caught, but I was completely indifferent. And just as I suspected, the day came. I was called into Human Resources with my manager. The call was replayed to me and I was asked for my input. Although there was some sadness and concern in the eyes of my manager and HR representative, both of whom had grown to know and support me, each one of us knew it was all part of the plan. As we said our goodbyes and I was offered personal support while I transitioned to my future endeavor, the atmosphere noticeably changed. The heaviness in my neck and shoulders grew lighter, like I just dropped a fifty-pound book bag. My manager escorted me out of the building and there was a rise in my spirit. An exciting chill ran across my body. I knew the Holy Spirit was right there with me, reminding me that God is always by my side during the good and the bad. Today was no different.

I walked to the parking deck and sat in my car. That's when reality set in. Being unhappy at your job is one thing, but being fired from that same job and having no backup plan was quite another. I had hit bottom. But I wasn't alone. His presence was still with me. Holding and comforting me. Letting me know that today was the start of that something wonderful and miraculous that I had envisioned. I glanced over at my vision board lying on the passenger seat. The scripture, Jeremiah 29:11, was staring back at me. Peace and contentment instantly overshadowed the fear, doubt, worry, and insecurity.

While God's presence offered me comfort, the truth was that I was petrified. Suddenly, my only stream of income was gone, I had kids to support and it appeared as if I was out of options. I supposed I could get another "dime a dozen" job to make ends meet, but how would another mediocre job be any different than where I was? What I needed was to get on with my dreams. I needed to figure out a way to make my vision board a reality. Then, a voice whispered to me, "You don't have to figure it out. Just trust me."

Immediately, what I saw through the fear was something I didn't expect. I could look at getting fired as an unfortunate event and a new reason to struggle; but, the longer I looked at it, the more I recognized it for what it really was. Getting fired was the wakeup call I needed to get on with my life's purpose. It was an "unwelcome at the time" push from God, letting me know that it was time, that I couldn't hold on to this mediocre position any longer. And there's a chance that, without being fired, I may have stayed at that job indefinitely. Thus, what I thought was my lowest point was actually the start of a whole new life and strengthening of my faith.

Yet, "faith without works is dead" (James 2:26). Accordingly, I set some new goals with my purpose in mind. I needed to enroll in school. That meant I needed to minimize my current expenses and pare them down to the bare bones. I paid off my car with my tax return, I got rid of the older two kid's cell phones and I eliminated every debt possible. We lived a "no frills" lifestyle off one income, student loans and tax returns, because I didn't want my studies to be distracted with work, and I managed our money impeccably because there was no room for error. We were functioning in survival mode in the present, but it was because I could see the bigger picture farther down the road.

Victory

Shortly after I enrolled in community college, I found out I was pregnant with our fourth child. Again, this was part of God's plan for my life. My pregnancy was here to help me prosper, not happening to harm me. I didn't drop out to focus on the baby. It was more important that I focus on what was going to make me a better mother in the long run. I stayed the course and finished nursing school in December of 2013. I was one of only two nurses in my class to participate in the graduation ceremony, but it was important that I walked across that stage - for my family and me. My graduation from nursing school was a testament to the sacrifices we all made for me to obtain my degree. It was my first degree, and my entire family was elated. That day will always be a memory that all of us - my children, my husband and me - can hold onto for years to come.

A few months after graduation, I scheduled the appointment to take my nursing licensure exam. I actually postponed taking it right after graduation due to fear and insecurity. Here again, fear crept in, aiming to discourage me and knock me off my plan to fulfill my purpose. As I sat in front of my computer, looking at Pearson's website, I reminded myself of how far I had come. The all-night study sessions, missed family functions, limited time with my husband and children, weight gain, anxiety, stress and dependency of loved ones to assist me with caring for my immediate family were part of the plan. I faced those obstacles head on with faith. This obstacle would be no different. I was determined to succeed, and that is exactly what I did.

Actually, the picture I am painting is not as pretty as the reality of the story. If you have taken a state licensing exam before, then you know the entire process is stressful. Its enough to throw you off your game. The staff is cold and stern, you are searched, your belongings are locked away and you can cut the tension in the room with a knife. After answering what seemed like a million NCLEX questions, my exam finally shut off and I was sent on my way with more anxiety. I had to wait to receive my results by mail, but luckily, I heard about a "trick" nursing students used to verify if they passed or not. I rushed to my car, whipped out my cell phone, and attempted it. At the time, I had an old school flip phone that allowed me internet access but didn't receive a good connection. I attempted to access the testing website, but I experienced problems maintaining an internet connection. As my frustration with my phone grew with the left-over anxiety of the test and the testing process, I started crying. The "trick" wasn't working for me and I started to tell myself I failed. I called my husband, crying, with tears streaming down my face all the way home. By the time I walked through the door, he had calmed my anxieties, and I was able to try the "trick" again from our desktop computer. And, it worked! I was in disbelief. I tried it again. It worked again! I yelled, hollered and screamed, "Hallelujah! Thank you, Jesus! It worked!" The house was immediately set in uproar. Everything was working in my favor. Praise, joy and excitement filled our home for days to come.

With the accomplishment of receiving my new license and title under my belt, it was time to find promising employment. But just because I was now licensed in my field, didn't mean that all the doors swung open for me to just walk through. Unfortunately, employment was not easy to find. I had the education I needed, but I didn't have any real experience, and I was unclear of exactly what my niche would be. I knew I loved helping people, especially helping young girls find their way, and I wanted to be able to incorporate that into my career. I also had an entrepreneurial spirit and didn't want to just be a cog in the giant hospital landscape. By this time, I had several vision boards hung along my bedroom wall. The one that stuck out the most was my very first one with my favorite scripture, Jeremiah 29:11. I glanced over that vision board and the many goals displayed that I had accomplished. The same calm and comforting voice whispered to me again, "You are not alone." I knew God would direct my path to greatness and lead me to where I should be.

After a few weeks of searching for employment, my college instructor sent me an email about a potential position working with children and adolescents in the mental health field. I applied and was offered the position. This position provided me with the opportunity to help kids and influence young girls, which was in line with my passion, so I soaked those aspects up. Later in my career, this position opened the door to more challenging positions in the mental health field and allowed me to obtain my nursing certification from the American Nurses Credentialing Center as a Psychiatric Mental-Health Nurse. Around the same time, the home care agency I worked for during my summer breaks from nursing school as a certified nursing assistant opened a part-time position for a registered nurse. I was offered the position and obtained a sense of pride from being able to work my way up within the agency and influence others to do the same. When I turned my fear of unemployment into hope of a prosperous future, I was blessed with two jobs in my career field. Look at God!

Greater

My passion has always been in holistic health and preventative care rather than focusing on disease management and illness. By extension, I also loved educating others on physical, mental, and spiritual health, and how it is all the components, working in conjunction with each other that comprise our total health. I believe optimal health and wellness allows us the opportunity to achieve our life's purpose. The home care position I maintained for years eventually was the key that opened the door to my developing a professional nurse coach practice. Providing one-on-one nursing assessments to my home care clients prepared me to offer personal and individualized health and wellness coaching to the community. Gradually, I was able to expand my business to offer first aid and CPR skills training and wellness products including therapeutic essential oils and aromatherapy jewelry. To this day, I believe God is preparing me to educate my community on a large scale, and I take whatever comes my way as a sign of this greater mission and my life's purpose.

One of those opportunities that came my way included speaking in front of large groups. As the educator of the agency's direct care providers and in-home aides, I was required to teach health care training skills on a regular and consistent basis. In order to be successful, I had to step out of my comfort zone in a big way. This was really difficult to do, but I relied on my faith to help me. I felt strongly that God wanted me to do great things with my career, and if I backed down from this challenge, I'd be rejecting my destiny. As I learned to step out of my comfort zone more and more and rely on my faith, a new scripture became my anchor and central in my life: "A man's gift maketh room for him, and bringeth him before great men." (Proverbs 18:16).

Since I received great feedback after my training classes and presentations, I knew I was on the right track and that if I could focus on this positivity, I could continue to increase my faith, minimize my fear and learn to be more comfortable in front of large groups. And that's exactly what I did.

Sometimes, when I'm at work doing what I absolutely love, I remember sitting at my old desk with my vision board in my peripheral vision. I remember how distant those dreams seemed at the time and that nagging feeling of uncertainty about my future. In those days, I couldn't even envision a path that would get me from that squeaky chair and dull building into the nursing field and doing what I loved, and it made my dream seem more daunting than it did possible. It could've been this uncertainty that made me cling so tightly to the job. After all - it's easier to hold onto your current reality than it is to imagine a new one, which is why I felt like I needed that unfulfilling job in order to survive.

But then again, I didn't need it. The scariest part was getting fired and having nothing left to cling to but my faith in God. It felt like a free fall, but little did I know that it was more like jumping from a diving board rather than blindly free falling. I wasn't falling to some horrid end with no control. I was diving into a luxurious pool of my choice. All I needed to do was trust that "God has good plans for me" and exercise my faith. Even though I felt like I was stuck in a limited position wasting my life away at a dead-end job, I was actually right where God needed me to be. I was suddenly in a position where my faith outweighed my fear. I was not alone. He was with me through the highs and the lows, and both worked to benefit me and my family in enormous ways.

Moreover, just like my vision board said, God knew the plans. I wouldn't come to any harm. I would prosper. And in front of me was a fabulous future that looked a heck of a lot like that old vision board on the corner of my desk…except now it was real and "exceeding abundantly above all that we ask or think" (Ephesians 3:20).

Biography

Raven Little is a native of Gastonia, NC where she lives currently with her husband, Reggett, and four children (Jasmine, Rashad, Jayden, and Chance). Raven and Reggett have shared the joys and pains of marriage and parenthood for over ten years.

Health and well-being is a passion Raven has carried in her heart since her early years, and a motivating factor in her return to college and nursing career. Raven graduated from Central Piedmont Community College in Charlotte, NC in December 2013 with an Associate Degree of Nursing.

After graduating from nursing school, Raven served the community in the mental and home health care fields. She began her career working in a psychiatric residential treatment facility with the child and adolescent population. This experience opened the door to work within the acute setting as a Psychiatric Nurse Assessor and Charge Nurse serving both the child, adolescent and adult populations. With three years of experience under her belt, Raven obtained her nursing certification from the American Nurses Credentialing Center as a Psychiatric Mental-Health Nurse.

While working to service the mental health needs of the community, Raven also serves the community as a home care nurse. Raven serves as Director for a local home care agency and utilizes her education and experience to educate her clients and staff on health and wellness within the home setting. She continues to service the community in this aspect conducting training classes and health and wellness coaching to meet the needs of her clients.

Raven believes, with all certainty, that God guides and orchestrates her path leading to her current position in her life and career. With a natural entrepreneurial spirit, Raven continues to serve the community as a Professional Nurse Coach, Home Care Agency Director and Staff Training Instructor, and Licensed Training Provider for the American Red Cross. Raven serves as an active board member for the Support Our Youth Services, Inc., a non-profit organization in her community.

Raven's mission is to provide holistic health care, coaching and education focused on the physical, emotional, social, mental, spiritual, and environmental aspects of well-being. She is passionate about raising awareness to preventative care and the practice of alternative therapies. Raven's care, coaching and education is current, relevant, and essential to living a healthy, active, and fulfilled life. Raven's vision is to inspire individuals to achieve their best health possible and create healthy communities collectively.

To contact Raven:

Email: ravenlittlernpllc@gmail.com

Facebook: facebook.com/ravenlittlernpllc

Facebook Groups: facebook.com/groups/thessentialife

Instagram: instagram.com/ravenlittlernpllc

Acknowledgements

I would like to thank my family and friends for believing in me when I didn't believe in myself especially my parents Lora C. Dobbins and the late Harold Dobbins Sr., who's love, and guidance were with me in anything that I ever pursued. In addition, I would like to thank my brother Dr. Harold Dobbins Jr and sister Dr. Omi J. Dobbins for creating the path and setting the bar high in education. Finally, my son, Stephon B. Smalls your birth both challenged and inspired me to be the best possible.

Joy

Through the Fire

By Joy Dobbins-Bostick, MSN, APRN-AGACNP, NRP, Author

Fire is a powerful, destructive force. I've seen fire ravage an entire home in minutes. It eats through the beams, the walls, the furniture, and the personal accents until there's nothing left behind but heaps of ash. For a home to remain standing after that or to come back from that type of damage is not an easy task. You can rebuild, but the scars remain. You can add layers of protection, but there is still worry. You can assume that the home is in the clear because it's already burned once, but you'd be wrong. You have to salvage any remains left behind and start new.

Fire coursing through a house is an apt analogy for the path my life has taken through the years. I started with a strong enough foundation. I grew up a part of a loving family in the suburbs. We weren't rich, but we had plenty. But for whatever divine reason, lots of fire and struggle continuously wreaked havoc on my foundation. Perhaps the struggle found me because I needed to be strong. Or maybe it found me because I needed to see for myself that nothing could keep me down. Whatever the reason, I had to dig deep for strength when I thought there was none left or else risk ending up a heap of ash myself.

As a kid, my answer to everything was, "I'm bored." The routine life of a student was never enough for me. I looked at the adults around me, and I knew I wanted to be grown. I wanted to live in the adult world where I was free to make my own choices, and I surely didn't want to be boxed into the schedule and trajectory that school laid out for me.

That's what probably led me to dating my classmate's brother. He was much older, so he had access to more of the freedom that I was craving. He graduated high school before me and joined the Navy. We had already talked about our future, and I felt like we are on the same page when we envisioned getting married and having kids someday. The vision of this future life together seemed to be everything I wanted, and my parents even approved of him.

But once he got his first job, he also got it in his head that he wanted to date people his own age. His timing was impeccable. He dumped me on my birthday leaving me devastated and crushed. Everything I had envisioned for myself and my future had gone up in smoke. Because I had placed all my value in what him and I were going to be together, it didn't seem like there was much hope left for me without him in the picture.

I knew where the pills were in my parent's medicine cabinet. So, I chased them with a glass of water. It seemed like the only solution for my broken heart.

I woke up in the emergency room where my aunt worked. Her friends at the hospital said that I could either have activated charcoal or have my stomach pumped, so I downed the charcoal like it was Kool-Aid, but there was nothing sweet left about my life. Any sugar dreams turned to shit in my opinion. My parents decided to send me to a mental facility. For them it was the answer, but to me it seemed like a futile waste of time. Group therapy was the bane of my existence, and I would do anything to miss it. I made some friends while I was there, and we became partners in crime. Whenever we got into trouble we would be kept out of group therapy, so it became our daily goal to stir up some mischief.

My friend used to urinate on herself as a form of spite and to prove that no one could control her. That display got her sent to the secluded dark room. A week later, her parents came and took her home because their insurance had run out. I remember asking if the same thing could happen to me, and the staff laughed in my face. They said, "Your parents have great insurance so you're going to be here for awhile." I didn't think that was funny.

Once I heard that however, I knew I had to make the best of things, but it was no easy task. And I didn't think any of the counseling they were providing was helping. It seemed to me that my doctor and I should switch places. He seemed crazier than I was, yet he was the one counseling me. As I continued the bland routine of counseling and group, I received a letter from my ex-boyfriend. I put off opening it for awhile, but finally opened it to find his words, "It's all for the best." I knew then I was on my own, and the only person I could rely on was myself.

Soon after, I was released and able to go back to my school. But being away for so long and in the place that I was, you don't just show back up like you were on an exotic vacation. I felt different, and it was like everyone could see right through me. Even though I kept to myself and tried to remain distant, minding my own business, everyone wanted to mess with the quiet girl. The thing about messing with the quiet girl though is that eventually the quiet girl fights back. But my retaliation only got me kicked out of school for fighting.

For a time, I attended an alternative school where I was doing well. The teachers were great, and I was thriving; but this fix was only temporary, and I had to go back to the school in my hometown.

Unfortunately, at this point my school district wouldn't take me back. My parents were at a loss of what to do. But my mom was resilient. She somehow managed to convince a superintendent from a different district to accept me into their school.

I latched onto this second chance. There was no way I was going to try to blend into the background again, so I resolved to get involved. I was going to take every opportunity to try to change a bad thing around. So, I joined the softball team. Things were looking up. I was playing first base and making friends. One day, my friends and I left school early to grab lunch. While we were out, the driver's car broke down. Luckily, we were close to his job, so he could simply walk to work, but my friend and I needed to get back to school. The driver asked his manager to take us back. The manager agreed to but only if one of us gave him our number. My friend claimed she couldn't because she had a boyfriend, so it fell on me if I was going to make it back to school before my Dad got there to pick me up for the day.

So, I made the connection, and gave him my number. I was reluctant at first, but things slowly progressed. He started bringing me lunch to school every day, and then taking me home after the school day ended. We went on a few dates, and even met each other's parents, but then one thing led to another, and I ended up pregnant. Planning for kids in the future with my previous boyfriend was one thing, but when it actually happens and you're in high school, it changes everything. I couldn't play softball anymore. I got behind in my classes, and then had to go to yet another school to be able to graduate on time. But even then, I was doing my best. I was a fighter after all. Now, in addition to being a fighter I was a mother, father, and I was trying to make things work. Or at least, I was trying.

While I was putting forth the effort to make things work, my boyfriend was in college pursuing other women. His pursuits were cut short when he was in a car accident, at least that's what I thought. He needed surgery and had a rod placed in his leg. I was doing my best to juggle everything that was going on, including caring for him. And in fact, I had just finished giving him a bed bath when the phone rang. He couldn't get to it, and asked me to pick it up. It was a female voice on the other end of the line. She immediately started questioning who I was, and I replied by telling her I was his girlfriend. And as a matter of fact, I was the mother of his child. She said they were together, and had no idea he was seeing someone else My heart broke yet again. I knew I had to move on. He didn't deserve me, and I didn't deserve having to put up with his extracurricular activities. We talked about it, and decided we would remain friends and co-parent as best as we could, but I was still broken.

I graduated high school, and was now ready to pursue my dream of becoming a nurse.

In 2002, I enrolled in nursing school for the first time and was set to pursue my dream. I also was propelled back into the dating game, that crazy rollercoaster of hit or miss encounters. The toughest part of which is keeping your heart open enough to notice or receive a good guy into your life while you're trying to protect yourself from the pain and heartache of opening up to the wrong person. It's a difficult balance.

Eventually I was introduced to a great guy, father of two, smart and able to provide. He taught me how to manage my finances, run a household, and entertain our friends. He was a great father to his own children, and took my son under his wing. We even got to travel and have fun amidst all of the work. But then the rug was pulled out from under me when I learned about his illegal income the hard way. He was keeping it from me and tried to discreetly make a drop while I was in the car with our dog. Apparently, he was being set up. I may not have known anything about his drug pursuits, but that doesn't matter to the arresting officers. We all slept behind bars that night – me, him and the dog.

I probably could've called my mom immediately to avoid having to stay overnight at the jail, but I was petrified to dial the numbers. I fell asleep picturing the disappointment and anger that would be written all over her face once I told her what I had gotten into now. It didn't matter that it wasn't my fault; somehow my choices led me here and the responsibility still felt like it sat with me.

Finally, though I worked up the courage to call my parents and they did come to my rescue. They brought an attorney who advised me to take a plea. It fell under the First Offender Act so rather than doing any time, I was put on probation and given an in-home curfew. It wasn't the ideal result, but I supposed it was the best I could hope for in my situation.

Months passed, and though my probation was moving along, other problems arose. My dad got sick, and my boyfriend broke up with me. I was so stressed out that my grades suffered. I couldn't focus, and I couldn't keep up with the work. I ended up on academic probation. Before long, I was kicked out of the program with no life plans, a sick father, and a broken heart. Nothing was going my way, but I still had a son to support. It was nearly impossible to see how my life could ever turn around.

Then a friend who had also gotten kicked out of the program told me that the fire department was hiring. I had no interest in being a firefighter whatsoever. I wanted to be a nurse, and it seemed like everything in my life was lining up to make that impossible. But I couldn't just think about the short-term. I had to provide for my son, and I needed any career that could help me do this. It wasn't about what my dream was in this moment; it was about doing what I needed to do to take care of my son. So, when the fire department called me in for training, I went. But that didn't mean that I didn't stop at my cousin's house every night in tears because the training was so difficult. I wanted to quit so badly.

One of the things that helped me get through this phase of my life was the presence of a good friend who was also a firefighter. We bonded watching fire movies, and everything seemed a little bit more manageable when we were together. It was typical for us to watch these realistic fire movies, and so one day, I turned on "Ladder 49" for us to watch. Interestingly enough, my friend couldn't seem to handle the movie and insisted I turn it off. I obliged, but made a mental note because the reaction was so odd. A week later, he went off to a fire, and never came back. He died of fire-related causes after responding to a call. Once again, I was devastated.

My father had been doing better with his emphysema for the past few years. He even got his wish of coming off the ventilator and was doing well. But about 3 months after my friend passed, my father lost his battle with emphysema.

I was dealing with two great losses and working 24 hour shifts at the fire station, but I was still committed to becoming a nurse and was working toward completing the nursing degree I had started so long ago. During this time, a fellow co-worker showed up and helped me cope with the loss of my father. We eventually ended up getting married. I was still working through a mountain of stress at this time. I was dealing with an abusive husband emotionally, mentally, then it became physically. I ignored all the red flags that were placed before me. I was blinded by a broken heart and was only worried about filling the void. My days went from the day to day battle of work and school to coming home to battle with my husband. I always imaged having the loving household that my mother and father had. I never saw my father hit my mother or never even heard my father raise his voice. I knew that I had to make some changes to my situation, so eventually we separated. Also, coupled with the long hours I was putting in at work and at school, I almost dropped out again. But this time I held on and finished my Associate's degree. Shortly after I got my Associate's, I enrolled in a program to get my Bachelor's in Nursing. And once I got that, I focused on getting my Master's.

This past year just four days after my birthday on June 24th, I went out for a drive on my motorcycle. It was a beautiful day, and I felt like celebrating with a ride. As I was enjoying the sun on my back and the breeze on my face, a car came out of nowhere and hit me full force. I never found out who it was because he or she fled the scene. This was a tough development because I needed multiple surgeries to recover. It was at this time, that I realized I needed a better way to earn money, so I started my own medical spa. Not only would this support me as I went through all the surgeries, but it was more in line with my passion and would allow me to eventually ease my way out of the fire department.

Throughout all of these hardships and struggles, I continued to persevere. And every time I persevere and come out the other end, I find myself stronger. With my Master's complete, I finally feel as if I'm on the path I was destined for. What's different about me now is that where there was once uncertainty, doubt and defeat, I've replaced with faith. I have faith that no matter what happens, I have the tools and resources to pick myself back up and turn it something positive.

My nursing degree will be a powerful addition to the business I've built. My son is 21, smart and healthy. He's seen what is mother has gone through, and is a better man for it. And I'm positive my Dad is looking down on me with nothing but pride. If there's one person who understood what nursing meant to me, it was always him. Perhaps I took a circuitous route to my dream, but I persevered and ended up on the other side, stronger and wiser because of every joy and every pain. Bitter waters truly are a blessing in disguise. And I wouldn't trade the path I took for an easier one because then I wouldn't be the person I am right now. I wouldn't have that extra bit of fight in me. I wouldn't have that extra touch of compassion with my patients, and I wouldn't have that resilience that is my foundation. I just wouldn't be me. And that would be the worst tragedy of all.

Biography

Unique experience that allows your image to speak to your soul. Services are provided by a Nurse Practitioner that takes pride in providing exceptional customer services. She is a native of the city she serves, she works as a Paramedic Sergeant for Atlanta Fire Rescue Department and a Paramedic Level III instructor. In addition, Joy has an outstanding academic background that includes two bachelor's degrees (BS in psychology from Argosy University and a BSN in nursing from Clayton State University) and a Master's of Science in Nursing from Walden University with a Major in Adult Geriatrics Acute Care Nurse Practitioner. She's been a nurse in several specialties to include Emergency Medicine, Neuro Step Down, Medical Surgical, Gastroenterology, and Aesthetics. She has extensive training and experience in providing antiaging treatments and specializes in skin rejuvenation and resurfacing. Also, she has experience with body sculpting, Botox, microblading, IPL (intense pulsed light) and so much more. She's passionate about educating other professionals in healthcare and business ventures. Also, she is the Co-Author of Glambitious Guide to Greatness "How to go from doubt to destiny & from surviving to thriving".

Contact:

Email: Joyastep@hotmail.com

Email: BelleJoiemedicalspa@gmail.com

Facebook: BelleJoieMedicalSpa

Instagram: @BelleJoie1

Joy Dobbins-Bostick
M.S.N. R.N. AG ACNP. BC. NP.

Acknowledgements

Dedicated to all the people who positively impacted my life and empowered me for greatness. Keep inspiring others to live in their truth.

To my mom: Thank you for your unwavering support. You are my hero.

To my sister: You contributed so much to my success. Thank you.

To Mea: Thank you for being my friend and always being there.

To my husband, Scott: I deeply thank you for your love and for being my protector. I love you.

Tamika

Metamorphosis

By Tamika Saunders, APRN, AGACNP-BC

I always knew I work in the field of helping people. It was a matter of how I would get there that always frightened me. I mean, considering my upbringing, there's no wonder my confidence in myself and what I could achieve was non-existent. My mother, a single parent, worked two full-time jobs to raise my sister and me. I saw her struggle, first hand, and I felt it, too. She would walk through the front door, tired and grimacing from standing on her feet all day. Yet, she still mustered the energy to cook a hot meal for us. I recall that sometimes there was barely enough food to make it through the next few days. However, my mom would find a way to put food on the table. I remember one house in which we resided that was not insulated, and quite frankly, unfit for winter conditions. My sister and I would huddle deep under thick blankets to escape the bitter low temperatures. My toes were numb. I would hold my urine to avoid meeting the relentless cold of winter that hovered over our beds. One morning, it was so cold that the water in the toilet was frozen. I was angry, frustrated and despondent. A feeling of determination and relentless desire to succeed ignited inside of me that morning. Something inside of me changed.

I grew up in a small town called Buena Vista, a city in Marion County, Georgia, with one stoplight. To put in perspective, in 2000, a census assessed that there were 2,000 people, 645 households and 377 families residing in the city. As you can imagine, everyone knew everybody. There was not much opportunity to succeed in Buena Vista. I dreamed of the day I would be able to pack my bags and set out into the world. Though I came from a small town, my goals were bigger than even I could have imagined.

As a child, my sister suffered from seizures. My family and I spent so much time with her in the hospital that I began to consider becoming a doctor, as we were constantly in contact with them. Over time, I became infatuated with the idea of going to college and someday becoming a physician. When the doctor asked my mother all the medications my sister took, she couldn't recall one particular medication. I, on the other hand, knew all of my sister's medications by name. I confidently interrupted with, "She takes Keppra!" The doctor was so proud of me for knowing the medication; he looked at me and said, "I think we have a future doctor here." That one statement sparked a fervent interest in the healthcare field. I even had the chance to care for my uncle who, after a car accident that resulted in a spinal cord injury, was permanently disabled and could not independently perform activities of daily living. I'd tie his shoes, help him wash up and did things that he couldn't. I began to enjoy the time I spent helping him - every day.

Years later, I had another encounter at a hospital. I was a cheerleader when I was 15, which required hours of intense practice and physical activity. As a result of all the hard work and training we did, I became dehydrated, fainted and was admitted into the hospital. While I was being treated, I realized that it wasn't the doctor who stayed at the patient's bedside—it was the nurse. Having that experience changed my idea of what I wanted to do as a career. I wanted to become a nurse. For me, being a nurse was about making people feel as cared for and as important as the nurses made me feel when I was a patient.

However, the odds seemed stacked against me. My grandmother, who lived in a shack with no running water and an outhouse in the backyard, helped raise us, since my mom spent so much time working. While my mother did her best, I didn't have a role model or a mentor that helped guide me into nursing school. So, before I even gave the idea of becoming a nurse some real thought, I almost gave up. College wasn't much of a possibly for me, or at least that's what I thought. It wasn't because my mother didn't value education, or want us to attend college; she just couldn't afford it. She was already working long hours, and, at one point, on welfare just to make ends meet, so college was, unfortunately, out of the question. Despite our financial status, I was determined to succeed. Just days after my high school graduation, I was packed and ready to leave Buena Vista. I moved to Boston with the intention of making a living for myself. I started working at a call center for a phone company. I knew college was expensive, but I was still determined to become a nurse, no matter what it took. I assumed I could get a job to pay my tuition; however, I quickly learned that life has a way of throwing curve balls your way.

After residing in Boston for a short time, I was called by my best friend, who was attending Albany State at the time. She told me that her grandmother wanted me to go to college and was willing to pay for my tuition. I was in shock. Tears of joy fell down my face. I finally felt like my prayers were being answered. I immediately moved back home to Buena Vista and started filling out the paperwork to apply for admission. I didn't know anything about applying to college. I knew very little about financial aid or that I could apply for funds to pay for school. There I was, sitting in the financial aide office, waiting for the financial counselor to give me the bill. I was nervous. My heart was racing. She extended her hand and gave me a piece of paper. While circling the bottom line, she stated that I would receive a refund from a Pell grant (I didn't even need my friend's grandmother's money!). I was officially enrolled in nursing classes at Albany State University. I walked anxiously to the nearby restroom, entered the stall, sat there and cried. I was overjoyed. Finally, I was taking the necessary steps toward realizing my dream of nursing.

My first year was perfect. I worked hard in school - I studied, was diligent and did well. I kept my eyes on the goal I had set for myself and was determined not to allow myself to be deterred by anyone or anything. Then came the second year. I started by first job in healthcare as a Medical Records Clerk. I made more friends and started attending campus parties. Why hadn't I learned, by now, that life throws curveballs that can derail even the most determined person?

During my sophomore year, I became pregnant with my daughter by my high school boyfriend. I was scared and disappointed. I knew that there was no way that I would be able to afford raising a baby while being away at school. I had to make some hard decisions. Ultimately, I moved back home and applied to a closer school so I could commute each day. I'd completed my prerequisites and was enrolled in the nursing program at Georgia Southwestern University. I gave birth to my beautiful daughter during spring break and was back in nursing classes in two weeks.

I attended my classes, but caring for my infant daughter while doing all the work and studying necessary to keep up in school, was much more difficult than I had anticipated. As time went on, my grades began to decline; I was failing several courses. Nursing courses were so difficult and the curriculum was rigorous. I went to see my advisor, who advised me to withdraw from the nursing program. In most nursing programs, failing one course means potentially being kicked out of the program, and then having to apply to another school, only to start from the beginning. That was not a viable option for me. Since I was failing several classes at that point, I took her advice. I withdrew from the program and switched my major to psychology, so I could graduate with my class, and because I knew I needed a degree to take care of myself. Withdrawing from the nursing program was one of the most difficult decisions I ever had to make. Here I was, with a small child, trying to get to a place where I could afford to take care of my daughter and myself. This was a major setback, and the second major obstacle I faced. I was depressed. Some days, I couldn't lift my head off the pillow. All I wanted was to be a nurse. I felt like a failure. I was embarrassed and painfully ashamed. How could I fail my daughter, my family, myself?

After graduating from Georgia Southwestern in 2005, with a bachelor's degree in Psychology, I moved to Atlanta. I knew that I would eventually go back to nursing school, but I wanted my daughter to be a little older before I tackled nursing curriculum again. In 2006, I got a job as a principal's administrative assistant at a high school in Atlanta. Providing for Tamea and me became impossible with just one job. The bills were piling up with no real solution in sight. I fell into depression again. I didn't share my hardships with anyone. My daughter moved to temporarily live with my mother two hours away. I was forced to get a second full time job. I was employed at a group home overnight. At the end of my shift at 7 o'clock in the morning, I showered there and then drove to my other full time job. Working 16 hours straight for months took a toll on me. My hair was fragile and thinned. I was anemic and extremely fatigued. I was getting nowhere fast. One day, I had to attend a school board meeting in downtown Atlanta, and on the way, I passed Grady Memorial Hospital. I saw so many nurses in scrubs and doctors in white coats walking across the street. At that moment, I said to myself, "What am I really doing? Why am I putting off my dream?" I remembered why I started, but most importantly, I knew why I had to finish. It was for Tamea. I made a promise that she would have a better childhood than what I experienced. Whatever sacrifices I had to make to earn that degree, I was willing to make them. I realized it wouldn't be easy, but I was positive it would be worth it.

That very same week, I tried to get into several nursing schools in Atlanta, but each school had a waiting list two to three years long. It was one roadblock after the next. I knew I couldn't prolong my goals for another two to three years without even knowing for sure if I would get into the program. What was I going to do? I decided to call my old nursing school, the program I had dropped out of, to see if I could re-enroll. My old advisor was still there and remembered who I was. She remembered my story and all I'd gone through. The same week I called, I was accepted back into the program at the very point where I'd withdrawn, which meant I didn't have to retake any courses. After ending the call, I let out a joyful cry and was filled with emotions! I resigned from my job and moved back to Buena Vista - yet another sacrifice - because there was little opportunity there. Finally, I was in nursing school again, and I thought everything from there would be smooth sailing. Tamea was older, so I was ready to ace the courses. Oh, was I wrong.

One day, we had an electrical fire, which caused an extended power outage and forced us to relocate. I was unemployed and couldn't afford a place to live. My daughter and I moved in with my best friend in a one-bedroom apartment. I felt like such a burden. After a few months, my sister was able to secure a nearby apartment, and we all moved in together. As if that wasn't enough, I failed the very first nursing course in which I enrolled. My heart shattered into a thousand pieces. Doubt began to invade my mind. Maybe I was away from college too long, or I wasn't smart enough to grasp the material, or maybe nursing was not meant to be. My heart told me differently. Two of my nursing professors encouraged me and gave me some tips on test taking. Although I would be behind my classmates, I retook the course. I passed, and eventually, I caught up with my graduating class. During the last semester of the program, while I was pregnant with my son, I scored in the 90th percentile on my exit exam and graduated in 2010 with my Bachelors of Science in Nursing. After many years of wishing, hoping, praying, struggling and sacrificing, I was a nurse. I did what seemed to be the impossible.

I knew what it was like to be poor and not have tangible resources. My childhood wasn't easy, and I was willing to do whatever I had to do to protect my daughter from the same struggle I experienced growing up. Tamea saved my life. She was the reason why I was willing to do whatever I needed to do in order to accomplish my goal. I knew my mother did the best she could for us. My mom taught me how to survive in the most vulnerable situations. I watched her fight for us. I wanted to give my daughter and son my best, too. Receiving my nursing degree was one of the most significant moments of my life. It taught me that no matter what obstacles you face, you can achieve any goal if you stay the course and have faith in yourself and in your abilities. I know that there is nothing in my path that I can't accomplish, because I've already accomplished so much. Giving birth to my son, Bryce, the same year I graduated made me work even harder. Tamea and Bryce are my heartbeats'…. S1, S2.

I practiced as a Registered Nurse for two years in Columbus, Georgia, a city that was close enough to Buena Vista that it allowed me to commute back and forth each day. Then, two years later, I moved back to Atlanta for greater opportunities for my family. In 2014, I was promoted to Director in Nursing Informatics - a great accomplishment for having only been a nurse for four years. That same year, I enrolled in graduate school. I worked full-time and successfully completed a master's degree as an Adult Gerontology Acute Care Nurse Practitioner. If someone told me that I'd eventually become a nurse practitioner, I wouldn't have believed him or her. It was a goal that seemed unreachable.

Today, I'm a wife, mother, author and nurse entrepreneur. I believe it is my life's work to help people. Every day isn't fun. Every patient isn't ideal. But I would not change anything about what I am doing, or the road I took to get here, because I know that I am living in my purpose as a nurse. I believe it is my will to inspire others like me. I want to encourage those behind me and be an example that anything is possible - that no goal is unattainable.

What would I tell an aspiring nurse today, especially those who think it's impossible, due to his/her economic status or hardships? I'd say, "Understand that poverty is a generational curse. Your grandmother may be poor. Your mother and father may be poor. However, you can break that cycle. You hold the pen to write your story." I wanted to create a better life for my family and myself. Once I realized the power of perseverance and self-motivation, doors opened. Goals were met but you have to do the work. Fight for your life, but fight for the lives of future generations, too. Let your life be its own perfect metamorphosis.

Biography

Tamika L. Saunders, a small town girl with humble beginnings, is a graduate of Walden University's Acute Care Nurse Practitioner Program, specializing in Adult Gerontology. She successfully obtained her BS in Psychology, followed by her BSN from Georgia Southwestern State University. Cardiology, Medical-Telemetry and Progressive Care are the many areas of nursing in which she has worked.

Today, Tamika has found success in her dream career; a loving family and a life well lived. After years of studies and countless hours on her feet as a nurse, Tamika embarked upon her first entrepreneurial journey with Priority Feet, a mobile foot care company created to bridge the gap between people with foot problems and overworked providers needing to focus on emergent foot care issues.

Now the founder of Nurses and the City, Tamika works tirelessly to promote work-life balance with the purpose of promoting events to create nursing scholarships. But her work doesn't stop there. Tamika is also an active member in her community of Alpha Kappa Alpha Sorority, Incorporated and known as Tamika Lynn, the co-host of Atlanta's hottest nurse radio show, Through the Lynns.

Tamika Saunders is a wife, mother, entrepreneur and author.

Acknowledgements

This book is dedicated to my three beautiful children: Amber, Jairus and Amira. And to my mom, Rosie. I know you all have watched me go to school for a long time. I know you thought it was easy but it wasn't. I want you to remember this; you can do anything you purpose in your mind.

Mom, I know I'm strong but I've always wondered where I got my strength from. One day, I realized I got it from you. You've endured so much in your life and you never complained. Thank you mom for being my strength!

I would like to say thank you to:

Dr. Orley Anderson, who assisted me with editing and formulating my ideas.

Front & Back Cover Photography: The LENNZ Photography with Thelennz Bennett

Makeup Artist: Sabrena L Powell-Cross

Hair: Dakota Atkins with La'Shae's Hair Salon

Book Cover: Candice Kilgore

Bridgette

Through Adversity to Triumph Victory in Nursing

By Dr. Bridgette Jenkins, DNP, MSN, RN

At my age, time has afforded me plenty of years to sit back and contemplate my life. When I was younger, I would only consider the hand that I was dealt. Believing that how things were, was just how things were going to be. But now, I meditate on the scripture, *"For I know the plans and thoughts that I have for you," says the LORD, "plans for peace and well-being and not for disaster to give you a future and a hope." (JEREMIAH 29:11 AMP)* What I finally realized is that God has always had a plan for my life. According to the scripture, God sculpted me with my future in mind. So, I accepted my life and pursued the dreams and desires that He had placed inside of me because they had purpose.

It all started when I was a little girl. I would go visit my grandparents in Mississippi. I watched my grandmother care for my ailing grandfather with such love and compassion that I was intrigued. It was then, at an early age, that I decided I wanted to be a nurse. Telling you that my journey to becoming a nurse wasn't easy would be an understatement. Truth be told, to get where I am, I've had to stare adversity right in the face! Advancing as a nurse and obtaining the highest level of education hasn't been easy. My journey has been filled with ups and downs, but I have been able to emerge a victor!

My journey started when I was 17 years old. I was young, pregnant and scared. Times were tough for me, and I had no hope. I didn't know what the future held, yet I was determined not to become the statistic everyone believed I would. I dreamed of being a better person and nothing was going to get in my way. My first encounter with higher education was a struggle. It was tough from the very start. I was in a terrible place with all that was going on, but I pressed my way. I found myself questioning whether I was ready for what I was getting myself into. I enrolled at an HBCU, where I would study pharmacy. I chose pharmacy because it was the closest degree to nursing that I could acquire. I wasn't ready. I was failing miserably. I had to drop out because of the struggles associated with being a teen mom. I was trying to figure out how to be an adult, a mother and a college student. It was really rough, but I was trying.

One day, I had a life changing encounter with myself. I sat down to thoroughly examine my life, asking myself profound, soul searching questions on what I needed and wanted out of life. That day, I made the courageous decision to live my life for me and my daughter who was about to celebrate her first birthday. I wanted to make life better for the both of us. I enrolled in the nurse aide program at the local community college. I knew I had made the right decision because I excelled without extreme effort.

I took small steps to reach my educational and personal goals. Obtaining my nurse aide certification laid the foundation for my journey to becoming a nurse. While continuing to work towards becoming a nurse, I faced many challenges along the way. My daughter was always sick. She suffered with severe allergies, colds, asthma and ear infections. As a result, I lost several jobs and I was kicked out of LVN school twice for missing too much time. The loss of income lead to my being evicted from my apartment. We had to stay at a homeless shelter and sleep in my car while awaiting my public housing voucher. I took a break from pursuing my nursing degree to get myself together and to nurse my baby back to health. While on break, I enrolled in an EMT program, which led to me getting a better job. I was able to get off welfare and start the pursuing my dream of becoming a nurse again. I believe that it's vitally important to follow your heart and pursue what makes you happy and fulfilled.

I worked hard to get in a nursing program. I was so excited about my future. I worked really hard to make good grades. Obtaining my Associates Degree in Nursing changed my life, as it opened doors of opportunity for me. I finally felt like I had made it. I was working in the profession I had dreamed of since I was a little girl…but I wanted more. I went back to school and continued my journey toward success by obtaining my Bachelor's Degree in Nursing. I had put in a lot of work and time on my journey from that scared little girl to becoming a nurse. Thinking back, things could have ended quite differently. I could have succumbed to my situation and became just another teenage statistic. But my determination to have a better life kept me going.

I had been working my dream job as a staff nurse in Labor and Delivery for eight years when I noticed that my vision was rapidly deteriorating. I had always worn glasses, but now it seemed like I needed new ones every six months. Soon, there was no way I could continue relying on upgrading glasses nor ignore what was going on.

After multiple visits to numerous doctors, I was diagnosed with an inherited degenerative eye disease called Stargardt's disease. Needless to say, I was devastated by the diagnosis. The doctors told me that most people with Stargardt's are usually blind by the age of 30. I was thirty-five at the time of diagnosis and, to add to my stress, I was in a bad marriage. I fell into a deep depression.

What was I going to do with my life? I never expected my life to take a turn like this. I had finally gotten my life together and everything had been working out for me… Now, it all seemed to be falling apart. Being a spiritual person, I screamed out to God. I asked, "Why me?" I just couldn't understand why I was being put through such an ordeal. I had done nothing to deserve this!

This was indeed a very sad time in my life. The more I thought about it, the more depressed I became. I had so many dreams and all of them were going to be just that - dreams. I was in a state of despair, but I decided that no matter what, I was going to enjoy my life. I told myself that I had not come this far, against all odds, to let myself be stopped by some disease or diagnosis. I had juggled all the curveballs life had thrown my way. This was just another one of those curveballs. I picked myself up from that despair. Though it was tough, I moved forward, choosing to look at life from a positive perspective.

Life continued as usual. My vision was stable and I was hopeful. One day while I was praying and meditating, I began to think about my future as a nurse. Labor & Delivery was a high acuity, fast paced and stressful area. I was thrown into anguish knowing that I would probably have to give up something I loved so very much. However, I wasn't ready to give it up. I couldn't go back home and wallow in gloom and despair. I started doing some research on Nursing with a disability. I found an organization called National Organization for Nurses with Disabilities (NOND). Their website had tons of information and resources for nurses and nursing students with disabilities. I spent hours reading articles and following links to other resourceful websites. I began to feel like there was still a place in Nursing for me, even with a disability. Since nursing is a very diverse profession, my choices were limitless. I began researching non-clinical areas in which I could practice nursing. There were so many options; *Certified Diabetes Educator, Medical Writer or Auditor, Patient Advocate, Legal Nurse Consultant, Informatics Nurse, Quality Improvement Coordinator and Educator - both clinical and non-clinical.* However, most of these positions required a master's degree in nursing or business management and/or special certification. Since I loved teaching my patients and the student nurses that rotated on our unit, I thought, "That's it - I'm going to teach!" How ironic that even in despair, we can find a glimmer of hope! With this goal in mind, I pushed hard, determined to get my master's degree so I could use my knowledge to educate others while practicing in my dream profession.

While enrolled in my master's program, I noticed that I couldn't see the board. So, I moved closer, but that didn't really help. I went back to the eye doctor to see if they could change my lenses again. It was then that my doctor told me that I was going blind and nothing could be done to stop it. This news broke me! I was angry, sad and everything in between. Every negative emotion that existed, I felt it. I had held on to the hope of a miracle. I had prayed that things would turn around and that I wouldn't go blind. I cried out to the Lord again, "The word says that you knew me before I was formed in my mother's womb, so you already knew I was going to go through this, so I trust you." I continued to fight on. I wasn't going to let this stop me. I was going to overcome this adversity, this challenge. I was going to achieve the goals and dreams that I had set for myself. Every last one of them.

I would be lying if I said it was smooth sailing. It was extremely tough for me especially with my health challenges. I had to work twice as hard as everyone else. I had to be patient with myself as well as learn to overlook the attitudes of others toward me. I also had to make some huge adjustments as a student. I had been a visual learner. However, since my visual acuity was getting worse, I had to adjust the way that I learned. I became an auditory learner.

I had to sit in the front of the class to avoid distractions, so I could listen intently. I met some naysayers along the way - people who couldn't understand why I wasn't home moping about my challenges. One nursing professor asked me, "What kind of work is a blind nurse going to do?" Another person asked, "Why are you wasting time going to school? You are not going to be able to work anyway." It was like I was back in elementary school being picked on by bullies. All of this made me question myself. What was I going to do? Was I fooling myself? Was it worth it? There were days I wanted to walk out of the classroom because no matter how close I sat to the board, seeing what was written there was impossible. Going through difficulties is something no one is ever ready for, especially when it seems there is no solution in sight (No pun intended). I thought of quitting, but I realized quitting wasn't worth it. I wasn't going to quit because people said so. I wasn't going to quit because my situation was trying to make me believe I should. No! I was going to continue to jump over the hurdles, even if it would take me longer to get over them. I was going to achieve every goal and dream I had set for myself… and I did!

Obtaining my Masters in Nursing Education opened doors of opportunity for me in nursing academia. I was hired to teach in a LVN and an ADN program…and I loved it! Every time I stood in front of a class, it felt so rewarding. I was mentoring students who were facing some of the same obstacles that I had faced. Despite all the things that had happened in my life, I was in a good place.

I recognized that I was enjoying life and finally, I was happy again.

This health challenge made me appreciate life even more. It helped me to see life differently. As a result, I became more patient and more understanding of people who struggle in their lives. It made me realize that it isn't over until you quit. The world might say you're done, but until you stop trying, you're still in the game.

Although I was enjoying life, I noticed I was experiencing headaches every day. Nothing I took or did relieved the pain. I went from doctor to doctor, trying to figure out what was going on. Even though I put on a brave front, I was terrified about what all of this meant. One doctor looked at my medical record and told me, "I'm sure you have multiple sclerosis." This was disturbing! In my mind I was screaming, "Not another devastating diagnosis!" Would it ever end? The doctor sent me to the lab to have blood drawn so she could confirm her diagnosis. I went, and I swear the technician took twenty tubes of blood. That evening when I returned home, I got in bed and stayed there for a week! I was emotionally drained from all the bad news and physically drained from all the blood that was drawn and from dealing with pounding headaches every day. Spiritually, I was empty, feeling like God had forgotten about me. There are moments when it seems like no matter how much you try to keep on pushing forward, life just keeps pulling you backwards. Life had finally taken its toll on me. I had put in so much work, but it seemed like nothing was working out as planned. I felt like the walls were closing in and there was no way out.

A week later, I returned to the doctor to get my lab results. My heart was extremely heavy as I sat in the doctor's office wondering what she would say. The doctor told me she had some good news and some bad news. She said I didn't have multiple sclerosis, which I was happy to hear. But, she went on to say that I did have two autoimmune diseases. She said I had Sjogren's; which is a chronic, slowly progressive, inflammatory autoimmune disorder. I really didn't know how to respond since I knew nothing about the disease. She also said I had Rheumatoid Arthritis; which is a chronic, debilitating autoimmune disease that affects the joints and certain organs. I went home and researched the diseases. That night, I cried myself to sleep.

With confirmation of these diagnoses, I started to change my mind set. If I was going to live life on my terms – my thinking had to change. Life had thrown me so many challenges and although I felt like everything was falling apart, there was no way I could give up. Life isn't easy, for most of us. We go through challenge after challenge, but we can't give up. I thought; as long as I am alive, there was hope. As long as there was breath in my body, I could achieve every goal I had set for myself. The challenges that I was facing were nothing but an attack, an evil plot or plan, I thought. They were not going to smother the fire that God had ignited in me when I was a little girl.

Despite all the negative things I was being told and how I was feeling, I started speaking positive things about my life and my health. I listened to inspirational audio books and watched videos which uplifted my spirit and caused me to grow closer to God. Surrounding yourself with positivity helps to eradicate the negativity, even if it's only for the moment. I told myself that I wasn't going to back down neither was I going to reside in sadness.

The headaches didn't go away. In fact, they got worse. But I pushed through them. I kept a smile on my face and I didn't let my situation get me down. I had gotten a very good job with one of the top nursing schools in my area. I was well on my way to achieving Dean or Director status. I loved my job and my students. I felt like I was living the life I wanted in spite of my health challenges. I continued to live life to the fullest. I spent a lot of time with my children, family and friends. I rode my bike, ran and walked for different organizations to raise money and awareness for various diseases. I took up new hobbies, went out more and began to meet new people.

Over the next two years, my health steadily declined, just as the doctors said it would. It was heart wrenching seeing myself become weaker and weaker, a mere shadow of who I once was.

Yet, I continued to try and live my life, making sure that my challenges didn't get the best of me. I felt very weak and the headaches were becoming more debilitating. I knew something was terribly wrong. Then it happened- I had a stroke. I woke up in ICU with everyone standing at my bedside. I could hear my mother crying and asking me to move my leg, but I couldn't. I tried and tried. That's when the tears began to flow. …But wait, there was some good news. Thanks to a dear friend for getting me to the hospital within the allotted timeframe, I received TPA and was expected to make a full recovery. The headaches I'd had for three years, were gone. After months of physical therapy, I was able to return to work and resume my normal activities. I do have one-sided weakness and a lazy eye because of the stroke, but I thanked God that I was still alive. Life was good, and I was grateful! I told myself that life was worth living and living was what I was going to do. I had put a lot on hold, but not anymore. It was time to go on living.

After graduating with my Master's degree, I thought I was done with school. I had been through so much, and I was tired. One of my colleagues had this bright idea of us obtaining our doctorate degrees. Our employer launched a new doctorate in nursing practice program and offered a discounted tuition program to all nursing faculty that applied and were accepted into the program. She thought that we should enroll because, in the very near future, a doctorate would be required to keep our positions, obtain tenure and acquire leadership positions in academia. I thought, "Girl, bye!" I didn't think I was ready for a whole new kind of stress. Before I knew it, we had applied and were accepted into the two-year program. I thought to myself, "You have lost your mind!"

But that didn't stop me from putting my best foot forward in this program. Whatever I do, I do it with excellence. Although it wasn't easy, I successfully completed the program. Obtaining my doctorate in nursing was, by far, the most difficult task of my life.

It was two years of me asking myself what had I gotten myself into.

While at the same time, working feverishly to finish what I had started. My health challenges during the program added to the difficulty. My physician was now telling me that I had "Lupus Syndrome." At first, I was in disbelief, but I pressed on toward my goal. I was plagued by severe pain, inflammation and fatigue for most of the program. There were times that I wanted to quit, but friends, colleagues and loved ones encouraged me to continue. It certainly was not an easy journey and I struggled quite a bit. Looking back, I can truly say, obtaining my DNP was worth all the hard work and every ounce of effort that it took.

Finally, I stopped crying and feeling like God had forgotten about me. He had been there all along, keeping me. It was His grace, mercy and favor that kept me through it all. Through my health challenges and struggles, I've come to realize that God knew exactly what He was doing. *"I am fearfully and wonderfully made..." (Psalms 139:14 KJV)* Though I still struggle with autoimmune issues, my vision has been stable for over six years. God is so good! My story is a testimony that with God, all things are possible. Nothing, not sickness nor disease, poverty, depression, loneliness, fear, financial hardships, teen pregnancy...

nothing and no one can keep you from reaching your goals. Health challenges, disabilities, adversities and other issues may make it difficult to achieve your dreams and goals. There will be times you may feel like quitting, but push through. There is a light at the end of the tunnel. Nothing can stop you, unless you allow it to. Trust me when I say I know what it feels like to experience moments of darkness, despair, anger and uncertainty.

I've learned to turn negative emotions into fuel. Let your setbacks and challenges motivate you to get up and work hard to accomplish your dreams and goals.

On this journey of reaching my goals, I have depended solely on God's grace and His mercy. I stood on His promises and my faith in Him. I found peace, purpose and strength in Him. I cannot forget about what I went through to get here. The process was for purpose. I'm charged with telling you, reminding you that you can make it. Trust the process. Don't ever give up on achieving your dreams. No matter what comes your way, don't quit. God can blow your mind and show His face through you. Who would have thought that I would have survived all that I've gone through, achieved all that I've set out to do and lived to give my testimony! I'm a witness that victory can be yours.

Biography

Dr. Bridgette Jenkins is a woman of God, Nurse, motivational speaker, educator, coach, prayer warrior, autoimmune disease warrior, mother, grandmother, friend, mentor, and minister of God's word. She is called to serve the people of God and she does it with love and compassion.

Dr. Bridgette Jenkins is a doctorally prepared registered nurse who specializes in education and community health. She has a heart for nursing students and those struggling to reach their goals. She mentors nursing students as they matriculate through the nursing profession.

She is the owner of Health Education Institute where she teaches lifesaving courses to healthcare providers and the public. Dr. Bridgette also speaks at churches and community events on various health and wellness issues that are prevalent among vulnerable populations.

She is the CEO/President of the Houston Chapter of Black Nurses Rock. A nonprofit organization committed to changing the lives of the citizens in the Houston area and the surrounding communities through service and education.

In her spare time, Dr. Bridgette can be found enjoying life with her beautiful family & friends. She can also be found participating in activities that bring awareness to diseases like; breast cancer, heart disease, lupus, diabetes, Alzheimer's, multiple sclerosis and diseases that cause blindness. She is a member of Sigma Theta Tau National

Nursing Honor Society, American Nurses Association, Texas Nurses Association and she serves as a Member at Large for The National Organization for Nurses with Disabilities (NOND) and as the NOND representative to the National Disability Leadership Alliance Steering Committee Task Force on Racism within the Disability Community.

Bridgette resides in Houston Texas where she's actively involved in her church and community. She is a mother to three adult children and a miniature schnauzer named

Dallas. She is also MiMi to two adorable grandsons.

Connect with Dr. Bridgette:

www.drbridgette.com

LinkedIn: Dr. Bridgette Jenkins

Facebook/Instagram: Dr. Bridgette

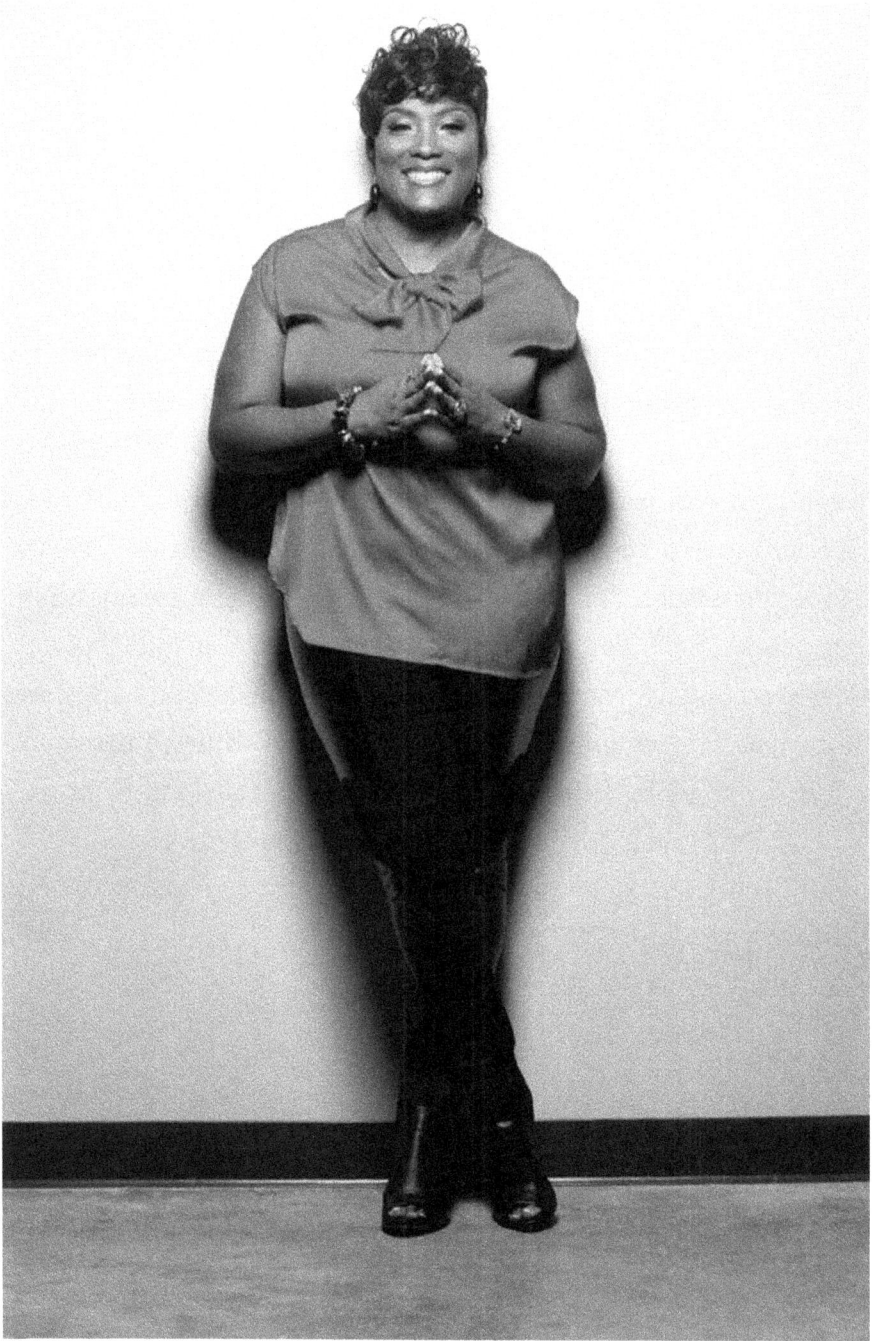

Acknowledgements

Gratefulness is the word that comes to mind when describing the transformation that has occurred in my life since becoming an author. It has been a blessing to allow my career as a Nurse catapult into other arenas in life. Albert, my wonderful husband, I appreciate you more than you will ever know. Your leadership, love and wisdom has supported me through the most enduring of times. Thank you to my beautiful children, Jon and Ali, I am so happy to have you in my life and I pray I make you happy and leave you a legacy to build. The My Heavenly Father, I thank you for loving me in spite of me. Thank you for this journey Lord, and may each day I conform more toward your likeness.

Michelle

The Nurse Echelon: A Victorious Nurse Anthology

By Michelle Greene Rhodes, MHS, RN, CCM, CMCN

The Echelon always existed as a place in my mind and as the place where all my hopes and dreams would be founded. You see, this was the place in my mind where it all began.

Ground zero. My first fistfight. A nearby neighborhood pool where I thought I was going to drown. This place where I was known as the "roller skate girl" and the place where I realized I lived in poverty. "Momma, is we poor?" My Mom, a.k.a. Ms. Mary, would never let me forget the day that I asked her that question. I never forgot it either. I always felt a little "mad inside" that we never had enough and, even if we were not poor, it sure felt like it. Not enough food, not enough money, not enough clothes… you get the picture. Government food, yes; the cheese, peanut butter and dry milk was our friend for quite some time. I was mad. The 1st of the month checks made us so happy for about a week or two, and then the struggle was real again. I had to get out; I had to move out towards something better.

Looking back, I think this is what lit my fire: promising myself, at age 8, that my children would not grow up "being poor" if I had anything to do with it. The joy that roller skates and dancing in the mirror brought me seemed to completely end at about age 12. That's when reality seems to hit us, right? Around that time, the late 1980's, teenage pregnancies were on the rise. All I could see were my "friends" getting pregnant in middle, and then high school, and this began to terrify me. There was NO way I was getting pregnant at an early age and end right back in the ghetto. Nope, not me. All I wanted to do was get a better life. My hopes and dreams came wrapped up in books and I saw them as the ticket to doing better. Mom had always taken me to the library on the weekends, so often I found myself going there to "getaway."

My parents were divorced when I was age 1, and my father only came around every blue moon. I would cross paths with him at my Grandparent's house, as I loved to go over there to hang out with my favorite guy, Granddaddy Clyde. Granddaddy told the most intriguing stories about growing up during the Civil Rights movement and about his many years working as a school janitor. Those were stories that I will never forget and that have affected my way of thinking for a lifetime. Meanwhile, my Dad was always so "busy" running his business that it seemed sometimes I was not a priority. I was mad about this, too. Mad that he always said, "We are gonna talk" every time I saw him, but the talks never happened. Well, when are we gonna "talk?" And what are we gonna talk about, anyway? I never understood why we couldn't just talk that minute. It was always going to happen later. I was mad about that. There were times when we did manage to spend time together, but it was always an argument because, deep down inside, I was mad that he wasn't there for me like I expected. To resolve that within my mind took me what seemed to be a lifetime. This "madness" almost drove me, literally, mad. You see, my Dad missed quite a bit of my life, in my opinion, from my middle school dance (for which my Mom made my fabulous outfit, by the way) to scolding my high school boyfriend. I mean, he was there for all of my graduations, but those were the happy times. The hard times were when I needed him most.

Now it was time to "find a husband;" not allowing God to lead me, I chose him on my own. It was time to fill that void in my heart that I carried for many years. So here I was, a new college graduate and happy that I had finally "made it." Enjoying my new nursing career, I felt ready to wed. Instead of finding myself and enjoying my independence, I ending up dating a guy that I met at a gas station who asked me for a hug. Yup. Sure did. He was cute and clever and seemed to have eyes only for me and I enjoyed it. We dated for four years after college and sought to marry. Then came the moment where he wanted to ask for my hand in marriage. Dad popped up really quick after hearing about it through family gossip. "Oh, I think we need to talk, son," he told my new fiancé, John. John was not afraid and went to the car where they stood for hours, talking. Eventually, John walked up to me, said "we are good" and that was about it. The next thing I knew, John and I were on an AIR JAMAICA jet taking off to Negril to wed in a beautiful manner that did not cost much. So, there was no Mother-of-the-Bride, no father walking me down the aisle. However, John's mother did fly over to attend. He had a close-knit family and so it was nothing for him to have support at any given moment.

Three years into the marriage, my son Jon Christian was born - a bright eyed, quiet soul that was inquisitive from the very start. The house had been built and the baby here. All should be perfect, right? Nope. We were dealing with our household demons. While everyone was only seeing things from the the outside, I was hurting inside. My marriage was failing due to money problems and alcohol. We both lacked discipline in those areas and life began to stress us out. My mother was dying and I didn't even know it. My father committed murder and was sentenced to life in prison. This would be the most trying time of my life. You see, I was happily serving my community as a Hospice nurse and felt I had finally found my "calling." One day it hit me - unless I cared better for myself, I would never be able to care for my patients appropriately. I listened to that still small voice and began to make some changes in my life. If I did not, I truly felt, at the time, that my life would be ending soon also. So, to divorce court I went, not sure of where else to turn. My parents had their own battles and, at this point, I was forced to make some big decisions on my own. Whatever I decided, they were supportive, but truly had no clue. How could I bother my mother with this when she had just suffered a massive stroke? My husband at the time had lost his father not long prior, so he just couldn't support me like I needed at that time. Or maybe my expectations were just too high? My only resolve, I thought, was to leave and start fresh - anew. I went to bankruptcy court alone; the divorce was final and the house went into foreclosure. I had no choice but to make better choices "next time," if the Lord granted me a next time. Prayer carried me through.

I moved back to my hometown with the hopes of a brand new start – a new apartment and a new federal job - things were looking up. My mom was placed in Assisted Living after her stroke and was stable. I also discovered my love for Coaching and Mentorship during this time when my boss, Barry, noticed my knack for leading teams and completing projects in excellence. I wanted to give my all to live this time around! I became certified as a Mentor that year, as well as completed Coaches training and Motivational Interviewing with Wellcoaches. I even got remarried to a wonderful man who was retiring from the Air Force and wanted to settle down. I thought all was well in my life. But no, there was more hell to endure first.

You see, I landed a promotion, for an additional $15K, in Texas. Since my ex-husband had been fired, wasn't working and had fallen behind paying child support, I ASSUMED this would be the perfect opportunity to not only make more money for my son and me, but also take my life to the next level. Naturally, everyone around me would benefit. It was never my intention to take my son to Texas and never come back. The Lord knows my heart and it was to work out any arrangements that we needed. I took the job and headed to Texas ahead of my son, as he spent summers with his Dad, and the VA needed an answer ASAP. It never entered my mind that he would not be joining me when school restarted. His Dad and I had discussed and agreed on the terms, but he somehow changed his mind. My baby had his room ready and the school was chosen. I had even enlisted him into Big Brothers for additional support. But the male judge back home said no. Our son would not be allowed to join me in Texas as it would disrupt too much of his life and was not in his best interest! What? How could he not see that this would be in everyone's best interest? Life threw me the biggest curveball I had ever known. I had lost custody of my child! I had the best lawyer, so I thought, and this happened to me! I was so crushed! I loved my baby boy with all of my heart and everyone knew that! I immediately put in for relocation back to Florida and visited home once a month until the relocation was granted. The nightly cries, sobs, loss of hunger and zeal for life…I don't think anyone will ever understand. This was the lowest point of my life. I kept my head up as best I could, even paid my ex-husband child support and wondered, "How much more, Lord?"

Six months later, the transfer with the VA Hospital was granted and I made it back home! I found a NEW attorney and was prepared to go back to court again to fight. Who knew that two weeks after returning to Florida, I would get the call of a lifetime! My ex-husband, John, had passed away at the age of 40. What in the world is going on in my life? Was I living underneath a curse right now? I felt as though the storm cloud would never lift. After all I had endured, it had come to this. Even to this day, I am shocked when I think about it. Nor do I know what was the cause of his death. I presume alcohol, but I will never know until Jon turns 18. Since I was no longer his wife, I didn't have access to that information. His mother told me at the hospital he died of "a broken heart."

The following year, my mother passed away from multi-organ failure. She had suffered not only the stroke, but was also found to have uterine cancer and brittle diabetes, and, although chemotherapy did not help the process, I honored her wishes of wanting to "fight at all costs." She had asked that I keep her alive and that I did. She fought until the end, until it was time for her to take her rest. Looking back, I see clearly that she set the tone for my life; she was my rock and my strength. Ms. Mary taught me how to endure until the end and never give up. As far as my Dad goes, I realized that this was a void that only the Lord could fill. I tried to fill it with books, jobs, travel and relationships, but none of that worked, and wisdom arrived the day that I realized that. I leaned and depended totally on my faith in God for everything, and no one could tell me anything differently. Tough times that don't kill you truly do make you stronger.

I am so thankful to my husband for enduring all of this along with me. He stuck right by my side and even testified in court as to our plans. I guess the Lord wanted this father and son to spend those final months together. That is the only thing that makes sense to me about this entire devastating situation in my life. If I had not had the Lord and Albert by my side, I am not so sure that I would have made it. They have a way of bringing peace to any situation that I might be going through. I thank God for his Spirit and I thank God for my husband keeping me during this entire life changing period.

After my ex and my mother took their final resting places, the flowers began to bloom again. My daughter, Ali, was born 9 months after my Mom died. Tell me God did not orchestrate the timing of my pregnancy! I was sent another fierce female to love and adore, just as my mom left! All of this seems so unreal, and as I face reality with each passing day, I see the overall plan here and it is beautiful. I now see the beauty in ashes.

My wisdom from these lessons in my life taught me this. Love hard, love true, love you. I say love hard because sometimes I think if I had not given up on my first marriage – if I had loved harder - maybe this all would not have happened. Of course, we will never know, but this next time I am going to love hard. Secondly, love true, meaning, love what truly makes you happy. No facades, no putting a face on, let it be real love. Lastly, love you! You see, it is LOVE that takes us to the "upper echelon." Not money, not houses, not cars…but truly loving yourself and others, as well as living a life of purpose. Had it not been for love, I would not have been able to find myself in the ups and downs. Oftentimes, we as women will place everyone and everything else first and barely make time for ourselves. I have had to learn a hard lesson about being diligent in my self-care regarding diet, exercise, spirituality and importance of family. I had to learn to make these things a priority for myself.

They say as we get older, we get wiser. That little girl from 483 Jordan Park Street South went through the ringer to learn the hard lessons on love that she didn't learn early in life - partially because of the lack of discipline that only a Dad can bring by being around and partially because I was an only child and a girl who did not want to listen to anyone. I have heard my heavenly Father's voice, my soul's cry and now I am able to join "The Nurse Echelon," one of the very few who truly walks in her purpose and passion. Empowering nurse entrepreneurs it what I love to do. It has been a joy to share my story and come together with these top notch ladies who, too, have loved themselves from the bottom to the TOP! *Fly high.*

Biography

Michelle serves as an Independent Coach and Consultant, offering Business Coaching to Nurses, having assisted 23 women into entrepreneurship in 2017. As a community servant, Michelle also serves on the Mayoral African American Advisory Council for the City of Tampa, and she also serves as the Co-Chair of Health with The National Coalition of 100 Black Women, Tampa Chapter.

In 2017, she has authored two books that offer advice for the Nurse Entrepreneur. She also serves as a Nurse Mentor strategizing on career, business, and life goals with her 6 Mentees.

Michelle is an active speaker at various healthcare workshops. Ultimately, her goal is to decrease the health care dollars spent while improving the quality of life for her clients, as well as assist nurses embrace their powerful knowledge and become entrepreneurs.

www.ingramcontent.com/pod-product-compliance
Lightning Source LLC
Chambersburg PA
CBHW071934090426
42740CB00011B/1694